Culinary Arts Institute

POLISH
COOKBOOK

Featured in cover photo:
a. **Pierogi, 36**
b. **Volhynian Beet Soup, 25**
c. **Stuffed Cabbage Rolls, 53**
d. **Kolacky, 67**

POLISH

POLISH COOKBOOK

The Culinary Arts Institute Staff:

Helen Geist: Director

Sherrill Corley: Editor

Edward Finnegan: Executive Editor • Charles Bozett: Art Director

Ethel La Roche: Editorial Assistant • Ivanka Simatic: Recipe Tester

Malinda Miller: Copy Editor

Book designed and coordinated by Laurel DiGangi and Charles Bozett

Illustrations by Joanna Adamska-Koperska

COOKBOOK

Culinary Arts Institute

1727 South Indiana Avenue, Chicago, Illinois 60616

Library of Congress Catalog Card Number: 76-14648
International Standard Book Number: 0-8326-0552-2

PHOTO ACKNOWLEDGMENTS
Cover photo: Bob Scott Studios
Inside photos: Zdenek Pivecka

We would like to acknowledge the advice and materials received
from the **Ladies Auxiliary of The Polish Museum of America**
and **West Jewelers** with regard to the photographs in this book.

CONTENTS

Introduction 7

Glossary 11

Appetizers and Canapés 13
      Appetizers 13
      Canapés 16

Soups and Stews 19
      Soups 20
      Stews 28

Breads, Noodles, and Dumplings 29
      Breads 29
      Noodles and Dumplings 30
        Pierogi 33
        Uszka 33
        Kołduny 34
        Naleśniki 34
        Kulebiak 34

Entrées 41
      Beef 41
      Fish 43
      Lamb 47
      Pork 48
      Variety Meat 49
      Main Dishes 51
      Poultry 53
      Game 56

Vegetables, Salads, Sauces, and Dressings 59
      Vegetables 59

Salads   62
Sauces and Dressings   63

Desserts   65

Easter   75
Easter Buffet   76

Christmas   85
Christmas Eve Dinner   86

Index   94

INTRODUCTION

Poland has brought special genius to almost every field of endeavor. Mikołaj Kopernik, better known as Copernicus, discovered that the earth revolved around the sun. Madame Marja Skłodowska-Curie was awarded the Nobel Prize in 1911 for her work on radium and its compounds. Joseph Conrad (called Teodor Józef Konrad Korzeniowski in his native Poland) gave many fine novels to English literature, and an indelible mark has been left on the history of music by Fryderyk Chopin and Ignacy Paderewski. American liberty was furthered by Tadeusz Kościuszko and Kazimierz Pułaski, the father of the American cavalry. Even in the field of nutrition Polish genius has had its effect: Kazimierz Funk, a Polish-American chemist, is credited with the discovery in 1912 of that organic substance now so much taken for granted: the vitamin.

CULINARY GENIUS

It should not be surprising, then, that a country that has produced these and so many other geniuses could also produce a cuisine of exceptional quality.

If this is your first venture into Polish cooking, you might expect it to closely resemble German or Russian cuisine. In a way, you are right. There are definite German and Russian (and French, Italian, and Jewish) influences in Polish cooking, but Polish genius has so modified these influences that a thoroughly distinct cuisine has been produced. You will often be tempted to say: "This tastes just like the French . . ." but before you finish the sentence you will realize that the food in your mouth is really unlike any you have ever tasted before.

Polish food is hospitable. It has the obvious hospitality of other cuisines: steaming and hearty *kluski z kapustą Polskie* (Polish noodles and cabbage) will warm you in winter and the unmatchable *chłodnik* (cold cucumber-beet soup) will cool you in summer—but Polish cuisine has a special hospitality all its own. Because of the special refinement it has

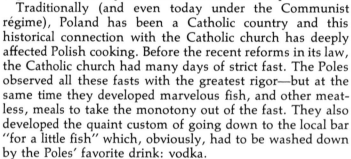

undergone, it is fragrant and aromatic but never overwhelming (except possibly, in quantity). It is a cuisine you can feel at home with.

Even more hospitable than their food are the Poles themselves. Their traditional greeting, *"Gość w Dom, Bóg w Dom"* (Guest in the house: God in the house), is more than polite sentiment; it is a strict norm for the treatment of all guests. At *Wigilia*, the most important meal of the year (eaten after sundown on Christmas eve), a place is always kept ready for a guest. During the rest of the year, although no special place is reserved, that feeling of welcome is still present. You are expected; there is always room for you.

HISTORY

The history of Polish cuisine parallels that of the nation itself. Polish history is a web of intermarriages with foreign royalty, conquests, partition, subjugation, and reconquests. Such foreign intervention at no time ever obliterated the Polish character of the nation but, necessarily, it did have a profound effect. The same is true of Polish cuisine. For example, intermarriages brought both French and Italian influence—the Italian, although unexpected, being the most striking. When Queen Bona Sforza married King Sigismund I in 1518 she brought chefs and gardeners from her native Milan. Their influence is best seen in the word used for vegetables: *włoszczyzna*, which means "Italian produce."

Traditionally (and even today under the Communist régime), Poland has been a Catholic country and this historical connection with the Catholic church has deeply affected Polish cooking. Before the recent reforms in its law, the Catholic church had many days of strict fast. The Poles observed all these fasts with the greatest rigor—but at the same time they developed marvelous fish, and other meatless, meals to take the monotony out of the fast. They also developed the quaint custom of going down to the local bar "for a little fish" which, obviously, had to be washed down by the Poles' favorite drink: vodka.

When the long fasts ended (forty days in Lent and four weeks in Advent, for example) the Poles celebrated with massive feasts. The plentifulness which is a characteristic of Polish cuisine can be traced to these happy occasions.

NATURAL RESOURCES

Polish cuisine, like all others, has also been determined by the natural resources of the country. The Baltic Sea and a network of rivers bring plentiful fish, especially the Polish favorite, the herring. Sausage and other meats have that distinctive Polish flavor because of the plentiful juniper wood used in the smoking process. Sour cream appears again and again in recipes due to the highly developed production of the dairy industry. It is a rare Pole who cannot distinguish all the varieties of mushrooms—an art learned as children on mushroom hunts. Mushrooms are therefore also very common in Polish cooking. That "Italian produce," the vegetable, is also found in kitchen gardens that dot the whole country. Always present in these gardens is the beet and that

most favorite of all Polish foods, the cabbage. Adam Mickie-wicz, in his epic poem *Pan Tadeusz*, extols these kitchen gardens:

> Beneath them was the vegetable bed.
> Bowing its bold and venerable head,
> A cabbage sat and seemed to meditate
> Here upon vegetables and their fate;
> There, its pods intertwining with the green
> Of a slim carrot's hair, a slender bean
> Gave it, from myriad eyes, a tender gaze;
> Here were the golden tassels of the maize;
> There a fat watermelon's belly rose
> Far from its parent stalk in snug repose,
> A ponderous guest among the crimson beets.
>
> *(Translated by Watson Kirkconnell, copyright by the Polish Institute of Arts and Sciences in America.)*

Wild game is also plentiful in Poland and much of it ends up in that marvelous national dish: *bigos*, or hunter's stew. Adam Mickiewicz's description of its preparation (again in *Pan Tadeusz*), although a bit too poetic for use in a recipe, is still mouth-watering:

> This bigos is no ordinary dish,
> For it is aptly framed to meet your wish.
> Founded upon good cabbage, sliced and sour,
> Which, as men say, by its own zest and power
> Melts in your mouth, it settles in a pot
> And in its dewy bosom folds a lot
> Of the best portions of selected meat;
> Scullions parboil it then, until the heat
> Draws from its substance all the living juices,
> And, from the pot's edge, boiling fluid sluices
> And all the air is fragrant with the scent.

DAILY ROUTINE

In the cities the average working hours are from seven to three-thirty. Breakfast is usually served at six-thirty, lunch *(drugie śniadanie)* at eleven, dinner at three-thirty or four, and supper at seven-thirty. Working hours on the farms are the same as those anywhere else in the world.

One delightful Polish custom is the break in the afternoon routine for a visit to one of the many tea shops *(cukiernie)*. If you order tea, it is brought to you in tall thin glasses. Sliced lemon is a more popular accompaniment than cream. If you prefer coffee, it is served in cups and topped with whipped cream. With your drink you can choose from an amazing array of pastries. There are wedges of torte filled with a deliciously rum-flavored nut filling *(tort orzechowy)*, or individually frosted rectangles or rounds filled with pure fruit flavors and marmalades. You may prefer cream puffs, Polish doughnuts *(pączki)*, or mazurkas *(mazurek)*. On your way out you can put a final touch to your break with sweet milk chocolate, fruit pastes, or bon bons.

MODERN RECIPES

You may be approaching Polish cooking with some apprehension. Is it too lavish? Will it take too much time to prepare? Can you easily obtain all of the ingredients? We at the Culinary Arts Institute have asked the same questions. We feel that this apprehension is probably the reason why Polish cuisine, although obviously excellent, is not very common (except in Polish homes) in America. We have therefore taken every effort to eliminate that apprehension.

Some lavishness was easily eliminated. Peacock pâté, for example, an old aristocratic recipe that requires the slaughter of 3,000 peacocks, did not demand much consideration, nor did other meals that require a week or more to prepare. In a more practical vein, we did control another example of Polish lavishness—that of the Polish serving. The Poles are very hearty eaters and a Polish serving is very likely to be much larger than an American serving. The servings given in this book will meet your expectations, not that of an army.

Beyond bringing the size of Polish cooking under control we have also, by diligent testing, brought you a rich cuisine that is matched to American kitchen equipment and that contains only those ingredients that are easily found in American markets. We have done this without sacrificing Polish tradition or that great Polish taste. Our testing is the guarantee.

Measurements are also given in terms that you will feel at home with (not in the "pinches" or "handfuls" so common in much ethnic cooking).

In a word, you can forget your apprehension. With this book you *can* cook the Polish way and be proud of the refined, hospitable taste you have created.

WYCINANKI

¼ actual size

A few words about the exquisite illustrations in this book are in order. They are based on the traditional Polish art form called *wycinanki*. Very thin paper, glossy on one side and dull on the other is doubled one or more times (for rectangles). The desired illustration is traced on the paper and then cut out with a scissors. The paper is then opened to show a "mirrored" illustration. Circles are done in the same manner except that the paper is usually doubled four times. The illustrations used in this book were not painted, but cut out and pasted down. Although many traditional designs are used, we believe that this is the first time that *wycinanki* have been used to illustrate actual recipes.

GLOSSARY

The following list of words and pronunciations will not make you into a Polish scholar but we thought that once you taste how delicious the recipes in this book are you might enjoy pronouncing some of them in their original language.

babki z wątróbek—*BOB-key zuh von-TRUE-beck*—liver cakes

baranina—*bah-rah-KNEE-nah*—lamb

barszcz z mięsa—*barsht zuh me-EN-sa*—beet soup with meat

barszcz klarowny—*barsht cla-ROV-ny*—clear beet soup

bażant pieczony—*BAAGE-ant pee-eh-CHOU-ny*—roast pheasant

bigos—*BEE-goes*—hunter's stew

budyń z szynki—*BOO-din zuh-SHIN-key*—ham pudding

buraki—*boo-RAH-key*—beets

chłodnik—*who-OWED-nik*—cucumber and beet soup

chrust-faworki—*ROOST fa-VOR-key*—favors

ciastka kruche—*CHAST-kah CREW-heh*—pecan cookies

ćwikła—*chu-VEE-kwah*—horseradish with beets

czarnina—*char-KNEE-na*—duck's blood soup

drożdżowe paluszki—*droge-JO-ve pah-LOOSH-key*—yeast fingers

dzika kaczka—*GEE-kah CAATCH-kah*—wild duck

galareta—*goll-are-RHE-ta*—gelatin

gęś lub kaczka duszona—*gensh lube CAATCH-kah doo-SHOW-nah*—stewed goose or duck

gołąbki—*go-WOMB-key*—cabbage rolls

gorace zakąski—*go-ROWN-seh zah-CONE-ski*—hot hors d'oeuvres

groch—*growh*—peas

grzanki—*guh-JOHN-key*—croutons

grzyby ze śmietaną—*guh-JI-beh zeh shmee-eh-TA-known*—mushrooms in sour cream

grzybki marynowane—*guh-JIP-key ma-ri-no-VAH-neh*—marinated mushrooms

grzybek ze słoninką—*guh-JI-beck zeh swo-NIN-cone*—mushroom with bacon

jabłka—*YAB-kah*—apples

jajka zawijane w szynce—*YAI-kah zah-vee-YAH-neh vuh SHIN-seh*—eggs wrapped in bacon

jarzyny—*ya-GIN-ny*—vegetables

kaczka—*CAATCH-kah*—duck

kanapki—*cah-NAP-key*—canapés

kapłon—*COP-won*—capon

kapuśniak—*kah-POOSH-ni-ak*—cabbage soup

kartoflane kluski—*car-toe-FLA-neh KLU-ski*—potato noodles

kiełbasa—*keh-BAH-sa*—sausage

kiełbasa w polskim sosie—*keh-BAH-sa vuh POL-scheme SO-sheh*—sausage in Polish sauce

kluski—*KLUS-ki*—noodles

kolaczki—*co-LATCH-key*—cookies

kołduny—*coe-DOO-ny*—stuffed noodle

kompot z malin lub truskawek—*COME-pot zuh MAH-lean lube trues-KAH-vek*—compote with raspberries or strawberries

krupnik—*CREWP-nik*—barley soup

kulebiak—*cu-LAY-bee-ack*—yeast fingers

kurczęta po polsku—*cur-CHEN-tah poh POL-scu*—Polish-style chickens

kuropatwy—*coo-row-POT-vy*—pheasant

kutia wigilijna—*CU-tia vi-gui-LEE-na*—Christmas Eve cookies

łatwy bigos—*WHAT-vy BEE-goes*—easy hunter's stew

legumina chlebowa—*leh-goo-MEAN-ah huh-leh-BO-vah*—bread pudding

makaron—*mah-KAH-ron*—noodles

marcepan—*mar-SEH-pahn*—marzipan

masło—*MAS-woe*—butter

mazurek—*ma-ZOO-rek*—mazurka

mizeria ze śmietaną—*mi-ZEH-ri-a zeh shme-TA-known*—cucumber salad

muchomorki—*moo-ho-MORE-key*—flybanes

naleśniki—*na-lesh-KNEE-key*—crêpes

pączki—*PONCH-ky*—doughnuts

pasta z kurzej wątrobki—*PAS-ta zeh CU-jay von-TROOB-key*—liver pâté

pasztet wieprzowy—*PASH-tet vi-ep-SHOW-vy*—pork pie

pieczeń—*pi-EH-chen*—roast

piernik—*pi-ER-neek*—ginger cake

pierogi—*pi-eh-ROE-gui*—pocket noodles

prosie pieczone—*PRO-sheh pi-eh-CHOU-neh*—roast pig

pulpety—*pull-PEH-ty*—meat balls

rosoł—*ROW-su*—bouillon

rosoł z kury—*ROW-su zuh CU-ry*—chicken bouillon

rosoł z mięsem—*ROW-su zuh me-EN-sem*—beef bouillon

rosoł z ryby—*ROW-su zuh RI-by*—fish bouillon

ryba zapiekana—*RI-bah zah-pi-eh-KAH-nah*—baked fish

sarna duszona—*SAR-na doo-SHOW-na*—stewed venison

sernik wielkanocny—*SIR-neek vi-el-ka-NUTS-ny*—Easter cheesecake

serowiec—*sir-OH-vi-ets*—cheesecake

śledzie—*SHLE-jay*—herring

szczupak—*shuh-CHEW-pack*—pike

tort orzechowy—*tort oh-jay-HO-vey*—nut torte

uszka—*OOSH-kah*—pocket noodles

wino—*VI-no*—wine

zacierki—*za-CHAIR-key*—quick noodle soup

zupa—*ZOO-pah*—soup

APPETIZERS AND CANAPÉS

Appetizers hold a very important place in Polish cuisine. The Poles are a very hospitable people and they look on a meal as more than a form of nourishment. A meal is an occasion, a time for entertaining, a time for conversation and laughter. It is no wonder, then, that appetizers are important. If you want a typical Polish taste and appearance, try Beet Relish for flavor and Flybanes as a platter decoration.

Pickled Mushrooms (Grzybki Marynowane)

4 pounds small mushrooms
4 cups boiling water
1½ tablespoons salt
Marinade:
1¾ cups water
15 peppercorns
2 bay leaves
2½ tablespoons salt
¾ cup sugar
¾ cup vinegar

1. Cut the mushroom stems off even with the caps.
2. Cook over medium heat in boiling water with salt until they sink to the bottom, about 10 to 15 minutes.
3. Remove mushroom caps; place in small sterilized jars.
4. Make marinade. Boil water with peppercorns and bay leaves for 30 minutes. Add salt and sugar. Stir until dissolved. Add the vinegar, bring to boiling.
5. Pour hot marinade over mushroom caps. Close the jars. Keep refrigerated 2 or 3 days before serving.

4 pints

Beet Relish (Ćwikła)

1 can (16 ounces) whole beets, drained
¼ cup prepared horseradish
¼ cup sugar
¼ cup vinegar
¼ cup water
1 tablespoon grated onion
1 teaspoon salt
⅛ teaspoon pepper

1. Grate or mince beets.
2. In casserole or other container with a cover, mix beets with remaining ingredients. Cover.
3. Store in refrigerator for at least 1 day before serving.

About 2 cups

Feet in Aspic (Galareta z Nóżek Wieprzowych)

1½ pounds pigs' feet or calves' feet
½ pound lean pork or veal shanks
3 carrots, pared
1 onion, cut in quarters
2 stalks celery or 1 small celery root
2 bay leaves
5 peppercorns
3 whole allspice
2 cloves garlic, crushed (optional)
Water
1 tablespoon salt
½ cup chopped fresh parsley
⅓ cup vinegar
Lemon wedges
Parsley sprigs

1. Have the butcher skin and split pigs' feet.
2. Cook pigs' feet, pork, vegetables, bay leaves, peppercorns, allspice, garlic, and water to cover in a covered saucepot 2 hours on low heat. Skim off foam and add salt, parsley, and vinegar; cook 2 hours.
3. Strain off the stock; set aside. Take out pigs' feet and carrots. Discard onion and spices. Dice meat and slice carrots.
4. Arrange sliced carrots on bottom of an oiled 2-quart mold. Put meat on top of carrots in mold. Add parsley. Pour stock into mold.
5. Chill until set, at least 4 hours. Skim off fat.
6. Unmold onto platter. Garnish with lemon wedges and parsley sprigs.

8 servings

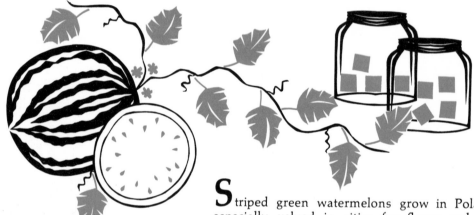

Striped green watermelons grow in Poland. They are especially valued in cities for flavor and color. Polish-American cooks sometimes adopt the thrifty customs of preserving watermelon rind in a sweet syrup.

Pickled Watermelon Rind

3 pounds watermelon rind
Salted water (use 3 tablespoons salt for each quart of water)
2 pounds sugar
3 cups distilled white vinegar
6 pieces stick cinnamon (3 inches each)
2 tablespoons whole allspice
2 tablespoons whole cloves
2 tablespoons whole mustard seed

1. Cut rind into 1-inch cubes; trim off outer green skin and bright pink flesh.
2. Soak overnight in enough salted water to cover. Drain.
3. Heat sugar and vinegar to boiling.
4. Tie spices in cheesecloth bag.
5. Add spice bag and melon rind to vinegar mixture. Cook, uncovered, until melon is transparent, about 45 minutes.
6. Discard spice bag.
7. If desired, add a few drops red or green food coloring to the rind.
8. Pack watermelon rind tightly into hot, sterilized jars. Pour boiling syrup over watermelon to within ⅛ inch from top, making sure vinegar solution covers rind. Seal each jar at once.

3 pints

Dill Pickles (Kiszenie Ogórków)

3 pounds 4-inch cucumbers
2 cloves garlic, crushed
1 cup distilled white vinegar
5 cups water
½ cup salt
3 tablespoons dried dill weed

1. Scrub cucumbers.
2. Place a layer of dill on bottom of a large ceramic bowl or crock. Cover with half the cucumbers. Add another layer of dill, then the remaining cucumbers. Add garlic. Top with a final layer of dill.
3. Mix vinegar, water, and salt. Pour over dill and cucumbers. Add more water, if needed, to cover completely.
4. Cover bowl with a china plate to hold pickles under the brine. Let stand in a cool place 4 days.
5. Seal in sterilized jars.

4 pints pickles

Fresh Mushrooms in Sour Cream
(Grzyby ze Smietaną)

1 pound fresh mushrooms, sliced
⅔ cup sliced green onions with tops
2 tablespoons butter or margarine
1 tablespoon fresh lemon juice
1 tablespoon flour
1 cup dairy sour cream
2 tablespoons chopped fresh dill or
    1 tablespoon dill weed
¼ teaspoon salt
⅛ teaspoon pepper
    Small rounds of rye or Melba
    toast

1. Sauté mushrooms and onions in butter and lemon juice for 4 minutes. Stir in flour. Cook slowly, stirring 1 minute. Add sour cream, dill, salt, and pepper. Cook and stir 1 minute.
2. Serve warm on toast.

About 2 cups

Pork Pâté (Pasztet Wieprzowy)

1½ pounds ground fresh pork
½ pound salt pork, diced
5 medium onions, quartered
2 pounds sliced pork liver
3 eggs, beaten
1½ teaspoons salt
½ teaspoon black pepper
1 teaspoon marjoram
½ teaspoon nutmeg
¼ teaspoon allspice
1 tablespoon beef flavor base
½ pound sliced bacon

1. Combine fresh pork and salt pork in a roasting pan. Roast at 325°F 1 hour, stirring occasionally.
2. Remove pork from pan and set aside. Put onions and liver into the pan. Roast 20 minutes, or until liver is tender. Discard liquid in pan or use for soup.
3. Combine pork, liver, and onion. Grind twice.
4. Add eggs, dry seasonings, and beef flavor base to ground mixture; mix well.
5. Line a 9×5×3-inch loaf pan (crosswise) with bacon slices. Pack ground mixture into pan. Place remaining bacon (lengthwise) over top of ground mixture.
6. Bake at 325°F 1 hour. Cool in pan.
7. Remove paté from pan. Chill.
8. To serve, slice paté and serve cold with **dill pickles** and **horseradish**.

About 4 pounds

Ham Pudding *(Budyń z Szynki)*

3 cups (about 1 pound) ground ham
2 cups warm unseasoned mashed
   potatoes
2 tablespoons melted butter
4 eggs, separated
1 teaspoon salt
½ teaspoon pepper
  Ham fat or drippings
  Fine bread crumbs
  Mustard Sauce (page 63) or
    Horseradish Sauce (page 88)

1. Mix ham and potatoes well.
2. Put butter and egg yolks into a small bowl of electric mixer; beat until thick and creamy.
3. Fold egg yolks into ham mixture; add salt and pepper.
4. With clean beaters, beat egg whites until stiff, but not dry.
5. Fold half of egg whites into the ham mixture; stir gently. Fold in the rest of the egg whites.
6. Grease a 1½-quart casserole with ham fat. Coat with bread crumbs. Spoon ham mixture into prepared casserole; cover.
7. Bake at 350°F 45 minutes.
8. Serve with sauce.

About 6 servings

Flybanes *(Muchomorki)*

8 hard-cooked eggs
4 small tomatoes
  Salt and pepper
  Mayonnaise
  Lettuce

1. Peel the eggs. Cut off both ends so eggs will stand evenly. Stand the eggs on a small tray; they will serve for mushroom stems.
2. Cut the tomatoes in halves lengthwise. Remove cores. Sprinkle with salt and pepper. Put each tomato half over an egg as a mushroom cap. Dot the caps with mayonnaise. Garnish the tray with lettuce.

8 flybanes

Ham and Egg Rolls *(Jajka Zawijane w Szynce)*

6 hard-cooked eggs
12 thin slices cooked ham
  Lettuce leaves
  Mayonnaise
  Pickles

1. Peel the eggs; cut in halves.
2. Roll each half of egg in a slice of ham. Secure with wooden pick.
3. Arrange lettuce leaves around ham and egg rolls on serving plate. Decorate with mayonnaise and garnish with pickles.

12 rolls

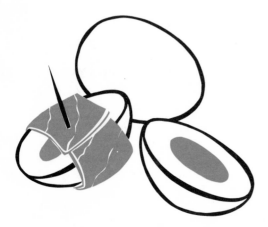

Canapés or *kanapki* are often set on a serving tray with no other garnish. They are served at afternoon tea, before dinner, and during parties.

BREADS

The bread foundations for canapés usually are white bread, fresh or toasted, and rye breads of many shades, plain or with caraway seed. Often crusts are trimmed off and the resulting squares are cut into triangles or smaller squares. Sometimes a cookie cutter is used to cut out rounds or other shapes from the bread slices. Occasionally French bread is used for canapé bases.

Polish cuisine uses a wide range of ingredients, but cabbage, beets, mushrooms, dill, and sausage are the most common.

SPREADS

Plain, sweet, unsalted butter is a favored spread for marrying base to topping. Flavored butter is a pleasing variation. Just a light film of butter, spread all the way to the edges, is adequate. It helps keep the bread fresh and attractive. Mayonnaise, cheese, and sour cream also may be used.

TOPPINGS

Vegetables: Small whole vegetables, boiled in herb-flavored chicken broth or pickled, make attractive toppings for canapés. Glaze with a light, chicken- or herb-flavored gelatin if desired.

Use tiny whole carrots or slices of carrots; Brussels sprouts; whole or sliced mushrooms; onions; beets; asparagus tips; artichoke hearts; whole or sliced cauliflower florettes. Slices of fresh, raw tomato or halved tomatoes can be used also.

Fish: Flaked, cooked fish or tiny fillets of cooked fish make excellent toppings for canapés. Garnish with capers or prepared beet horseradish. Use a savory butter spread on French bread.

Anchovy fillets, either flat or rolled with capers, are excellent as garnish or topping.

Caviar, red as well as black, is tasty with a garnish of sieved hard-cooked egg. Just a dot of caviar on top of slices of salmon or chicken makes an elegant canapé.

Pickled herring, herring in cream, and all the endless varieties of herring beloved by Poles are excellent canapé toppings. Pickles and onions complement herring.

Eggs: Hard-cooked eggs, sliced, sieved, halved, or quartered, make colorful garnish or topping for canapés. Use patience and a sense of design. Exercise creative skills in separating yolks from whites. Make borders, spoke designs (using chopped parsley or dill), or fill the inside of a cucumber or tomato slice with its seeds removed.

Other toppings: Use meat, poultry, or fruits to increase the colorfulness and variety of a canapé tray.

Various other cold hors d'oeuvres, or *zimne zakąski,* are popular at Polish gatherings. Relishes, pickles, olives, bite-size pieces of sausage on skewers, spices, oysters, cold tongue, shrimp, and steak tartare are all delightful possibilities.

Hot hors d'oeuvres, or *gorace zakąski,* are easiest to make by choosing compatible combinations in canapés which can be quickly broiled or heated in the oven.

Mustard Butter *(Masło Musztardowe)*

½ cup butter (at room temperature)
½ cup prepared mustard

1. Beat the butter with the mustard until creamy.
2. Spread on toast rounds to serve with **sardines** or **herring.**

1 cup

Easy Hunter's Stew, 28, here cradled in a Polish china tureen, is a simplified but succulent version of the national dish, Bigos.

Onion-Chive Butter
(Masło Szczypiorkowe lub Koperkowe)

1 tablespoon sliced green onion
1 tablespoon snipped chives
½ cup butter (at room temperature)

1. Blend onion, chives, and butter.
2. Form into a roll about 1 inch in diameter. Chill.
3. Cut into small disks.

About ⅔ cup

Spring Cottage Cheese Spread
(Twarożek Wiosenny)

1 carton (12 to 14 ounces) cottage cheese
½ cup dairy sour cream
8 radishes, shredded
3 tablespoons sliced green onion
½ teaspoon salt
Lettuce leaves
Radish roses
Rye or French bread

1. Mix cottage cheese with sour cream. Add radishes, onion, and salt; toss to mix well.
2. Mound on lettuce leaves. Garnish with radish roses. Surround with bread.

About 2⅓ cups

Chicken Liver Spread (Pasta z Kurzej Wątróbki)

½ pound chicken livers
1 cup milk
¼ cup rendered chicken fat or margarine
1 medium onion, cut in quarters
3 hard-cooked eggs, peeled and cut in half
½ pound cooked ham or cooked fresh pork, cut up
¼ teaspoon salt
¼ teaspoon pepper
⅛ teaspoon garlic powder (optional)

1. Soak livers in milk 2 hours. Drain livers and discard milk.
2. Melt fat in skillet. Add livers and onion and cook over medium heat until tender.
3. Combine livers, pan drippings, and all remaining ingredients. Grind or mince.
4. Add extra melted chicken fat or margarine, if desired, to make spread of desired spreading consistency.

About 4 cups

Purée of Anchovies (Purée Sardelowe)

1 can (2 ounces) flat anchovy fillets, drained
3 slices stale white bread
Water
½ cup dairy sour cream or mayonnaise
1½ teaspoons vinegar

1. Mince or pound anchovy fillets.
2. Moisten bread with enough water to cover; then squeeze dry. Break into bits or mince with a fork. Blend in sour cream and vinegar to make a smooth purée. Serve as a spread with dark bread rounds.

About 1 cup

SOUPS AND STEWS

Soup is basic to the Polish meal; it is to the Poles what rice is to the Oriental and pasta to the Italian. Cold Cucumber-Beet Soup is a specialty in summer, Duck Soup in winter; Borscht is common all year round. You should also try the Nothing Soup—at least as a conversation piece. Bigos is the Polish national dish. You will have to go a long way to find a heartier, more fragrant stew.

Bread Kvas

1 quart hot water
1 pound beets, pared and sliced
1 rye bread crust

1. Pour hot water over beets in a casserole. Add bread. Cover with a cloth. Let stand 3 to 4 days.
2. Drain off clear juice and use as a base for soup.

About 3 cups

Beet Kvas

5 to 6 cups boiling water
3 cooked beets, sliced
½ cup vinegar

1. Pour boiling water over beets; add vinegar. Let stand at room temperature 2 to 4 days.
2. Drain off juice and use as a base for soup.

About 4 cups

Rye Flour Kvas

4 cups rye flour
6 to 8 cups lukewarm water

1. Put flour into a crock and gradually mix water into flour until smooth and the consistency of pancake batter. Cover with a cloth.
2. Keep in warm place 48 hours. Mixture will bubble. When brown liquid comes to top and bubbling stops, it is done. Skim off foam.
3. Fill crock with cold water; stir. Flour settles to bottom in a few hours. Pour off clear liquid and refrigerate in jars.

About 6 cups

"Nothing" Soup (Zupa Nic)

4 eggs, separated
⅓ cup sugar
1 quart milk
½ teaspoon vanilla extract
¼ teaspoon salt
  Dash of cinnamon or nutmeg
    (optional)

1. Beat egg yolks with 3 tablespoons of the sugar until very fluffy.
2. With clean beaters, beat the egg whites until frothy. Gradually beat in the remaining sugar. Continue beating until stiff, not dry, peaks form.
3. Heat milk over medium heat in a deep 10-inch skillet or 5- or 6-quart Dutch oven just until a "skin" forms on top, about 3 minutes.
4. Drop beaten egg whites by rounded spoonfuls into hot milk. Cook until the egg white "kisses" are set and firm to the touch, about 5 minutes. Remove kisses with a slotted spoon to waxed or absorbent paper.
5. Stirring constantly, gradually add hot milk to egg yolks. Strain into a heavy saucepan. Add vanilla extract and salt. Cook and stir over medium low heat about 3 minutes, until thickened, and soup coats a spoon.
6. Serve soup with 2 or 3 meringues in each portion. Sprinkle with cinnamon, if desired. Serve hot or cold.

4 servings

Pumpkin Soup (Zupa z Dynią)

1 quart milk
1 can (16 ounces) pumpkin
½ teaspoon allspice
¼ teaspoon nutmeg
¼ teaspoon pepper
½ teaspoon salt
1 cup cooked rice
2 tablespoons butter or margarine

1. Beat milk into pumpkin in saucepan. Stir in spices and salt. Bring just to boiling.
2. Stir in rice and butter. Cook and stir 5 to 10 minutes, or until rice is heated through; do not boil.

8 to 10 servings

Mushroom Soup (Zupa Grzybowa)

1 carrot
2 sprigs parsley
1 stalk celery
2 small onions, sliced
1 teaspoon salt
2 cups water
½ pound fresh mushrooms, sliced,
    or 2 cans (4 ounces each)
    mushrooms
1 cup water or mushroom liquid
1 teaspoon dill weed
1 teaspoon chopped parsley
1 tablespoon flour
¼ cup cold water
½ cup dairy sour cream or whipping
    cream

1. Cook carrot, parsley, celery, 1 onion, and salt in 2 cups water 20 minutes. Strain; discard vegetables.
2. Cook mushrooms and remaining onion in ½ cup water 8 minutes. Add to the vegetable broth along with ½ cup water, dill, and parsley.
3. Mix flour with ¼ cup cold water. Stir into soup. Bring to boiling. Cook and stir 3 minutes. Remove from heat.
4. Beat in sour cream. Serve hot.

About 4 servings

Duck Soup *(Czarnina)*

1 duck (5½ to 6½ pounds), cut up
1 quart duck, goose, or pork blood
1½ pounds pork loin back ribs
2 quarts water
2 teaspoons salt
1 stalk celery
1 sprig parsley
5 whole allspice
2 whole cloves
1 pound dried prunes, pitted
½ cup raisins
1 small tart apple, chopped
   (optional)
2 tablespoons flour
1 tablespoon sugar
1 cup whipping cream or dairy
   sour cream
   Salt, pepper, lemon juice, or
   vinegar

1. Purchase duck and blood from butcher. The blood will contain vinegar. (If preparing your own poultry, put ½ cup vinegar into glass bowl with blood to prevent coagulation. Set aside.)
2. Cover duck and back ribs with water in a large kettle. Add salt. Bring to boiling. Skim off foam.
3. Put celery, parsley, allspice, and cloves into cheesecloth bag and add to soup. Cover and cook over low heat until meat is tender, about 1½ hours.
4. Remove spice bag from kettle. Discard bones, cut up meat. Return meat to soup. Add prunes, raisins, and apple (if desired); mix. Cook 30 minutes.
5. With beater, blend flour and sugar into cream until smooth. Then add blood mixture, a little at a time, continuing to beat.
6. Add about ½ cup hot soup stock to blood mixture, blending thoroughly. Pour mixture slowly into the soup, stirring constantly until soup comes just to boiling.
7. Season to taste with salt, pepper, and lemon juice or vinegar. Serve with homemade noodles, if desired.

About 2½ quarts

Note: If a thicker soup is desired, increase flour to 3 to 4 tablespoons or add 1 cup puréed prunes.

Dill Pickle Soup *(Zupa Ogórkowa)*

4 large dill pickles, diced or
   thinly sliced
2 tablespoons flour
2 tablespoons butter or margarine
3 cups meat broth, bouillon, or
   meat stock
⅔ cup liquid from pickles or water
2½ cups cubed boiled potatoes
   (optional)
1 cup dairy sour cream

1. Coat pickles with flour.
2. Melt butter in a large skillet. Add pickles and stir-fry over medium heat 3 minutes.
3. Stir in beef broth, pickle liquid, and potatoes, if desired. Cook over medium heat 15 minutes, stirring occasionally.
4. To serve, mix in sour cream or spoon dollops of sour cream into each bowl before ladling in soup.

About 6 servings

Kohlrabi Soup *(Zupa z Kalarepy)*

5 cups meat broth or bouillon or
   meat stock
1 pound kohlrabi, peeled and diced
2 tablespoons water
1 tablespoon cornstarch or potato
   flour
1 teaspoon salt
¼ teaspoon pepper
1 tablespoon butter, melted
2 egg yolks

1. Boil broth and kohlrabi in large saucepan. Cover; reduce heat and simmer 20 to 30 minutes, until kohlrabi is tender.
2. Mash or purée the kohlrabi.
3. Make a smooth paste by stirring water into cornstarch. Add to soup. Season with salt and pepper. Cook soup over medium heat until it boils.
4. Beat melted butter into egg yolks. Then beat in a little of the hot soup.
5. Remove soup from heat. Beat in egg yolk mixture. Serve hot with **croutons.**

About 8 servings

Barley Soup *(Krupnik)*

1 cup pearl barley
2 quarts meat stock
¼ cup butter or margarine, cut in
    pieces
2 carrots, diced
2 potatoes, diced
4 ounces (canned or frozen)
    mushrooms, sliced
1 stalk celery, chopped
    Giblets from 1 chicken or
      turkey, diced (optional)
1 teaspoon dried parsley flakes
1½ teaspoons salt
½ teaspoon pepper
1 cup dairy sour cream (optional)
    Sprigs of fresh dill

1. Combine barley with 1 cup of the meat stock in large saucepan. Bring to boiling; reduce heat and simmer until all stock is absorbed. Add butter piece by piece, stirring.
2. Boil vegetables and, if desired, giblets in the remaining stock until crisp-tender. Then add barley, parsley, salt, and pepper. Cook until barley is tender.
3. Garnish each serving with sour cream, if desired, and dill.

About 2½ quarts

Black Bread Soup *(Zupa Chlebowa)*

2 cups stale dark bread pieces (rye
    or whole wheat)
2 medium onions, quartered
1 carrot, quartered
1 leek, sliced
3 sprigs parsley
½ cup cut fresh or frozen green
    beans, lima beans, or peas
1 stalk celery, sliced
1 celery root or parsnip, sliced
1½ quarts water or meat broth or
    bouillon
1½ teaspoons salt
½ teaspoon pepper
    Dash nutmeg
1 cup milk or water
3 egg yolks (optional)
    Croutons or sliced hard-cooked
      eggs (optional)

1. Combine bread, all vegetables, and water in a 3-quart saucepan. Simmer 30 or 40 minutes, or until vegetables are tender.
2. Purée vegetables by pressing through a sieve or using an electric blender. Add vegetable purée to broth in pan. Stir in salt, pepper, nutmeg, and milk. Cook until soup simmers; do not boil.
3. If using egg yolks, beat them and then stir in a small amount of hot soup. Immediately beat mixture into soup. Remove from heat.
4. Serve hot with croutons or sliced hard-cooked eggs, if desired.

About 6 servings

Caraway Soup *(Zupa Kminkowa)*

5 cups meat broth or bouillon or
    meat stock
2 tablespoons caraway seed
2 tablespoons browned flour (see
    page 56)
2 tablespoons melted butter
½ pound diced cooked or smoked
    kiełbasa (Polish sausage) or
    salami (optional)
    Buttered croutons
    Dairy sour cream (optional)

1. Rapidly simmer broth with caraway seed 15 minutes. Strain and discard seed.
2. Blend flour into butter until smooth.
3. Return broth to saucepan. Stir in flour mixture and sausage. Bring just to boiling, stirring.
4. Serve garnished with croutons and, if desired, sour cream.

About 6 servings

Sauerkraut Soup *(Kapuśniak)*

2 pounds pork shanks, ham hocks, or pigs' feet
1 quart water
1 medium onion, sliced
1 bay leaf
5 peppercorns
1 sprig parsley or ¼ teaspoon dried parsley flakes
1 pound sauerkraut
2 cups meat broth, bouillon, or meat stock
8 to 12 ounces bacon or smoked link sausage, diced (optional)
¼ cup raisins or 2 tablespoons sugar (optional)
3 tablespoons lard or margarine (at room temperature)
3 tablespoons flour
½ teaspoon salt
¼ teaspoon pepper

1. Cook pork shanks in water in a 5-quart kettle 20 minutes. Skim off foam. Add onion, bay leaf, peppercorns, and parsley. Cook about 45 minutes, or until meat is tender.
2. Remove meat from broth. Strain broth; return to kettle.
3. Remove meat from bones; discard skin and bones. Dice meat.
4. Rinse sauerkraut with cold water; drain.
5. Add diced meat, drained sauerkraut, beef broth, and if desired, bacon and raisins to kettle. Simmer 1 hour.
6. Mix lard and flour to a smooth paste; stir into simmering soup. Cook and stir over medium heat until thickened. Mix in salt and pepper.
7. Serve with plain boiled potatoes or potato dumplings, if desired.

About 10 servings

Fish Broth *(Rosół z Ryby)*

1 large onion, quartered
2 tablespoons butter or margarine
½ small head savoy cabbage
2 carrots, cut up
2 celery stalks, cut up
1 parsley root, cut up
3 quarts water
6 peppercorns
1 bay leaf
Salt
2 pounds fish fillets
1 teaspoon lemon juice
1 teaspoon salt
½ teaspoon nutmeg

1. Brown onion in butter in a small skillet.
2. Meanwhile, simmer the vegetables in water with peppercorns, bay leaf, and salt to taste 15 minutes.
3. Add onion and fish to vegetables; simmer about 10 minutes, or until fish flakes easily.
4. Remove fish and vegetables. Use for another dish, if desired, or discard.
5. Strain broth. Add lemon juice, salt, and nutmeg.
6. Boil broth rapidly 10 minutes. Strain again, if desired. Serve as a clear soup.

About 2 quarts

Chicken Broth *(Rosół z Kury)*

1 chicken (3½ pounds)
2 teaspoons salt
7 cups boiling water
2 carrots
¼ small head savoy cabbage
2 stalks celery
1 parsley root (optional)
1 large onion, quartered
5 whole peppercorns
1 tablespoon chopped parsley

1. Simmer chicken with salt in boiling water 30 minutes.
2. Add carrots, cabbage, celery, parsley root (if desired), onion, peppercorns, and parsley.
3. Remove chicken. Strain broth. Quickly chill broth, then skim off fat. Store broth in refrigerator or serve hot with dumplings.
4. Use chicken meat for other dishes. Fat can be used in cooking instead of butter.

About 1½ quarts

Meat Broth *(Rosół z Mięsa)*

2 pounds beef shank or short ribs,
    or pork neckbones
1 pound marrow bones
3 quarts water
1 large onion, quartered
2 leaves cabbage
2 sprigs fresh parsley or 1
    tablespoon dried parsley flakes
1 carrot, cut up
1 parsnip, cut up
1 stalk celery, cut up
5 peppercorns
1 tablespoon salt

1. Combine beef, bones, and water in a 6-quart kettle. Bring to boiling. Boil 15 minutes, skimming frequently.
2. Add remaining ingredients. Simmer rapidly about 1½ hours, or until meat is tender.
3. Strain off broth. Chill quickly. Skim off fat.
4. Remove meat from bones. Set meat aside for use in other dishes. Discard bones, vegetables, and peppercorns.
5. Return skimmed broth to kettle. Boil rapidly about 15 minutes, or until reduced to about 6 cups. Store in refrigerator until needed.

About 1½ quarts

Meat Stock: Prepare Meat Broth as directed. Chill. Lift off fat. Boil until reduced to 3 cups, about 45 minutes.

Borscht with Meat *(Barszcz z Mięsa)*

¼ pound salt pork, diced
1 large leek, thinly sliced
1 medium onion, sliced
1 celery or parsley root (about 6
    ounces), peeled and cut in
    thin strips
3 beets (about ½ pound), peeled
    and shredded
½ head cabbage (about ½ pound),
    thinly sliced
2 quarts water
1½ pounds cooked meat such as
    kiełbasa (Polish sausage),
    ham, beef, or pork, diced
1 can (8 ounces) whole tomatoes
1 cup Rye Flour Kvas (see page 19)
2 tablespoons butter (at room
    temperature)
2 tablespoons flour
1 teaspoon salt
½ teaspoon pepper
1½ tablespoons lemon juice or
    vinegar
1 cup whipping cream or dairy
    sour cream
    Prepared horseradish (optional)

1. Fry salt pork until golden in a 5-quart kettle. Add leek and onion. Fry until onion is transparent.
2. Add celery root, beets, cabbage, water, and meat. Cook until celery root is crisp tender; about 25 minutes.
3. Add tomatoes and kvas; mix. Cook over medium heat 30 minutes.
4. Make a smooth paste of butter and flour; stir into the simmering soup. Cook and stir until soup thickens. Add salt, pepper, and lemon juice; mix.
5. To serve, spoon a small amount of cream and horseradish into each bowl. Ladle hot soup into bowl and stir to blend with the cream and horseradish.

About 2½ quarts

Volhynian Beet Soup (Barszcz Wołński)

¼ cup dried navy or pea beans
2 cups water
2 cups Bread Kvas (see page 19)
2 cups meat broth, bouillon, or
    meat stock
6 medium beets, cooked and peeled
1 can (16 ounces) tomatoes
    (undrained)
1 small head cabbage (about 1½
    pounds)
1 small sour apple
    Salt and pepper
1 tablespoon butter (optional)
    Dairy sour cream

1. Bring beans and water just to boiling in a large kettle. Remove from heat. Let stand 1 hour. Then boil for 20 minutes, or until beans are tender. Add kvas and meat broth.
2. Slice beets. Mash tomatoes or make a purée by pressing through a sieve or using an electric blender. Add beets and tomatoes to beans.
3. Cut cabbage into sixths; remove core. Pare apple, if desired; core and dice. Add cabbage and apple to beans.
4. Season to taste with salt and pepper. Stir in butter, if desired. Cook soup over medium heat 30 minutes.
5. To serve, spoon a small amount of sour cream into each bowl. Ladle in hot soup and stir.

About 2½ quarts

Fresh Cabbage Soup
(Kapuśniak ze Świeżej Kapusty)

5 slices bacon, diced
1 pound cabbage, chopped
2 carrots, sliced
2 potatoes, sliced
1 stalk celery, sliced
1½ quarts water
2 tablespoons flour
2 tablespoons butter or margarine
    (at room temperature)
    Salt and pepper

1. Fry bacon until golden but not crisp in a 3-quart saucepan.
2. Add vegetables and water. Simmer 30 minutes, or until vegetables are tender.
3. Blend flour into butter; stir into soup. Bring soup to boiling, stirring. Season to taste with salt and pepper. If desired, serve with dumplings or pierogi.

6 to 8 servings

Cold Cucumber-Beet Soup (Chłodnik)

1 small bunch beets with beet
    greens (about 1 pound)
1½ quarts water or chicken broth
1 teaspoon salt
2 medium cucumbers, pared and
    diced
6 radishes, sliced
6 green onions with tops, sliced
2 tablespoons fresh lemon juice
2 cups dairy sour cream or
    buttermilk
1 dill pickle, minced (optional)
3 tablespoons chopped fresh dill
    or 4 teaspoons dill weed
    Salt and pepper
1 lemon, sliced
2 hard-cooked eggs, chopped or
    sliced
12 large shrimp, cooked, peeled,
    and deveined (optional)

1. Scrub beets and carefully wash greens. Leave beets whole; do not peel. Put beets and greens into a kettle with water and salt. Bring to boiling. Cover. Reduce heat, and cook slowly until tender, about 30 minutes, depending on size of beets. Drain, reserving liquid in a large bowl.
2. Peel and chop beets, mince the greens.
3. Add beets and greens to reserved liquid along with cucumber, radish, green onion, lemon juice, sour cream, pickle (if desired), and dill. Season with salt and pepper to taste; mix. Chill.
4. Serve garnished with lemon slices and hard-cooked egg and, if desired, whole shrimp.

About 2 quarts soup

The spelling varies in Yiddish and Russian, but to the Poles, it is Barszcz Polski, a beet soup made with the clear liquid from fermented beets or rye flour. The strong, sour, fermented liquid is kvas; neither vinegar nor lemon juice truly approaches this flavor.

Clear Borscht (Barszca Klarowny)

1 cup Beet Kvas (page 19)
5 cups meat or vegetable broth (or use 3 beef and 3 vegetable bouillon cubes dissolved in 5 cups boiling water)
2 tablespoons brown sugar
Dairy sour cream (optional)

1. Heat kvas and broth to boiling in a saucepan. Skim surface if necessary.
2. Serve hot or chilled with **rye bread** and a large dollop of sour cream, if desired.

About 1½ quarts

Wine Soup (Polewka z Wina)

1 quart white wine
2 cups water
1 piece cinnamon stick (3 inches)
3 whole cloves
3 whole allspice
5 egg yolks
2 tablespoons sugar

1. Bring wine, water, and spices to boiling. Strain; discard spices.
2. Beat egg yolks with sugar until thick. Slowly add the hot wine mixture, beating constantly until a thick foam forms at the top. Be careful not to curdle the yolks by pouring hot wine too fast. Serve in cups with **wafers.**

8 to 10 servings

Beer Soup (Polewka z Piwa)

2 cans (12 ounces each) beer
3 egg yolks
4 teaspoons sugar
Croutons or grated cheese

1. Bring beer to boiling.
2. Meanwhile, beat egg yolks with sugar until thick.
3. Stirring constantly, gradually add a small amount of beer to egg yolks. Then carefully stir egg yolk mixture into boiling beer, reduce heat, and stir 1 minute; do not boil.
4. At once remove from heat. Serve with hot croutons.

About 4 servings

Apple Soup (Zupa Jabłkowa)

6 large apples (see Note)
1 quart water
¾ cup sugar
½ teaspoon cinnamon (optional)
½ cup lemon juice
1 cup whipping cream
⅔ cup white wine (optional)

1. Pare and core 5 apples. Cook in water until soft. Rub through a sieve, or purée in an electric blender to make an applesauce.
2. Combine applesauce, sugar, and cinnamon (if desired) in a large bowl.
3. Shred or mince remaining apple; mix with lemon juice. Stir into applesauce mixture. Chill.
4. To serve, blend cream into applesauce mixture. Stir in wine, if desired.

8 to 10 servings

Note: If desired, substitute 1 can or jar (16 ounces) applesauce and 1 cup water for apples and water.

Prune Soup *(Zupa z Suszonych Śliwek)*

1 package (12 ounces) pitted dried
    prunes
3 cups hot water
½ pound rhubarb, cut in pieces
2 cups boiling water
½ teaspoon cinnamon
¼ teaspoon cloves
⅔ cup sugar
1 tablespoon cornstarch or potato
    flour (optional)
¼ cup cold water (optional)
¾ cup dairy sour cream
    Cooked macaroni or croutons

1. Soak prunes in 3 cups hot water 1 hour. Cook in the same water 3 to 5 minutes.
2. Cook rhubarb in 2 cups boiling water 10 minutes.
3. Combine cooked fruits; press through a sieve, or purée in an electric blender.
4. Combine purée in a saucepan with cinnamon, cloves, sugar, and, if desired, a blend of cornstarch and cold water. Bring to boiling, stirring constantly. Remove from heat.
5. Cool slightly; beat in sour cream. Mix in macaroni. Or top with croutons and serve after the meat course.

8 to 10 servings

Plum or Apricot Soup *(Zupa ze Śliwek lub Moreli)*

1 pound fresh apricots or plums
1 quart water
1 tablespoon potato flour
⅓ cup sugar or ½ cup apricot or
    plum jam
    Peel and juice of ½ lemon
    (optional)
¼ teaspoon salt
1 pint dairy sour cream
    Buttered croutons

1. Cook fruit in water until tender, 20 to 30 minutes.
2. Discard pits. Purée fruits by pressing through a sieve or using an electric blender. (Fruit may be pitted raw for easier handling, but the taste will be less subtle.)
3. Stir potato flour into liquid in which fruit was cooked. Bring to boiling, stirring until thickened.
4. Pour thickened liquid into fruit purée. Stir in sugar, lemon peel and juice, if desired, and salt. Cook, stirring, 3 minutes.
5. Serve hot or cold. Spoon sour cream on top of each serving of soup. Garnish with croutons.

8 to 10 servings

Berry Soup *(Zupa Jagodowa)*

1 quart fresh blueberries,
    blackberries, raspberries, or
    strawberries; or 2 packages (10
    ounces each) frozen berries
1 cup fresh currants (optional)
2 cups water
1 tablespoon cornstarch or potato
    flour
2 tablespoons water
    Peel and juice of ½ lemon
⅔ cup sugar
½ teaspoon cinnamon or ¼
    teaspoon cloves
1 pint whipping cream or dairy
    sour cream

1. Using a potato masher, crush 3 cups of the berries in a large kettle. Reserve 1 cup berries for garnish. Purée fruits by pressing through a sieve, or use an electric blender.
2. Add the 2 cups water; simmer 15 minutes.
3. Mix cornstarch with 2 tablespoons water. Stir in soup. Bring to boiling, stirring until soup thickens.
4. Stir in lemon peel and juice, sugar, and cinnamon. Chill.
5. To serve, beat in cream. Or spoon soup over dollops of sour cream. Garnish with reserved whole berries.

6 to 8 servings

Cherry Soup (Zupa Wiśniowa)

3 pints pitted fresh red tart cherries
or 3 cans (16 ounces each)
pitted red tart cherries, drained
½ teaspoon cinnamon
¼ teaspoon cloves
1 quart water
½ cup sugar
¾ cup dairy sour cream
Cooked noodles or croutons

1. Combine cherries, cinnamon, and cloves with the water in large saucepan. Bring to boiling. Reduce heat and simmer 15 minutes.
2. If desired, purée fruits by pressing through a sieve, or use an electric blender.
3. Add sugar and stir until it dissolves. Cool thoroughly.
4. Beat in sour cream. Serve with noodles or croutons after the meat course.

8 to 10 servings

Hunter's Stew (Bigos)

6 pounds diced cooked meat (use at
least ½ pound of each of the
following: beef, ham, lamb,
sausage, veal, pork, venison or
rabbit, wild duck, wild goose,
or pheasant)*
5 ounces salt pork, diced
1 onion, minced
2 leeks, minced
2 tablespoons flour
1 pound fresh mushrooms, sliced,
or 3 cans (4 ounces each) sliced
mushrooms (undrained)
1 to 2 cups water or bouillon
6 pounds sauerkraut
2 teaspoons salt
1 teaspoon pepper
2 teaspoons sugar
1 cup Madeira

1. Fry salt pork until golden but not crisp in an 8-quart kettle. Add onion and leeks. Stir-fry 3 minutes. Stir in flour.
2. Add mushrooms with liquid and water to kettle; simmer 5 minutes.
3. Drain and rinse sauerkraut. Add to kettle along with cooked meat, salt, pepper, and sugar. Cover; cook over medium-low heat 1½ hours.
4. Stir in wine. Add more salt, pepper, and sugar to taste. Simmer 15 minutes; do not boil.

12 to 16 servings

*If meat must be prepared especially for this stew, each piece should be braised separately. Put meat, poultry, or game into a Dutch oven with 1 carrot, 1 stalk celery, 1 onion, 1 parsnip, 1 clove garlic or 1 sprig parsley, 5 peppercorns, 1 cup water, and 1 cup wine. Simmer, covered, until meat is tender.

Note: When wine is added, chopped apples, heavy cream, and/or cooked small potatoes may also be added.

Easy Hunter's Stew (Łatwy Bigos)

¼ cup all-purpose flour
1 teaspoon paprika or caraway
seed
2 tablespoons butter or margarine
1 pound lean beef, cubed
1 pound lean pork, cubed
2 pounds sauerkraut, rinsed and
drained
2 medium onions, sliced
12 ounces kiełbasa (Polish sausage)
or 6 smokie link sausages, cut
in 1-inch pieces
1 can (4 ounces) sliced mushrooms
(undrained)
½ cup dry white wine
Chopped parsley (optional)
Small boiled potatoes (optional)

1. Combine flour and paprika; coat meat pieces.
2. Heat butter in a Dutch oven or saucepot. Add meat and brown on all sides. Add sauerkraut, onion, sausage, mushrooms, and wine; mix. Cover and cook over low heat 1½ to 2 hours, or until meat is tender.
3. Remove meat and vegetables to serving platter. If desired, garnish with parsley and serve with small boiled potatoes.

6 to 8 servings

BREADS, NOODLES, AND DUMPLINGS

Pierogi is a word that makes a Polish mouth water. It will do the same for you. This pocket-noodle can be filled with meat, cheese, potatoes, sauerkraut, or even fruit. Uszka, kołduny, naleśniki, and kulebiak, which can also be filled, are delicious variations of pierogi. Liver Mounds are a special taste treat and, of course, you must have dark rye bread as an accompaniment to any Polish meal.

Dark Rye Bread

2 cups milk, scalded
2 tablespoons butter
2 tablespoons sugar
1 teaspoon salt
1 package active dry yeast
½ cup lukewarm water
4 cups rye flour
2½ cups whole-wheat flour
2 tablespoons caraway seed

1. Pour scalded milk over butter, sugar, and salt in a large bowl; stir. Cool.
2. Dissolve yeast in lukewarm water.
3. Add softened yeast and 3 cups rye flour to milk mixture. Beat thoroughly, then beat in remaining rye flour.
4. Cover and let rise in warm place until doubled in bulk. Turn onto well-floured surface. Knead in whole-wheat flour and caraway seed. Knead until dough is smooth.
5. Divide dough in half and shape into 2 round or oblong loaves. Place round loaves in greased round pans; oblong loaves in greased loaf pans. Cover and let rise in warm place until doubled in bulk.
6. Bake at 450°F 15 minutes; reduce heat to 350°F and bake 35 to 40 minutes longer. Brush with melted butter 5 minutes before done if a more tender crust is desired.

2 large loaves

Croutons for Fruit Soups

4 stale dinner rolls or slices baba
   or bread
½ cup whipping cream
2 tablespoons butter or margarine
¼ cup confectioners' sugar

1. Cut rolls into 1-inch cubes.
2. Dip cubes in cream; quickly sauté in butter.
3. Dust with confectioners' sugar.

About 14 to 18

Croutons *(Grzanki)*

2 slices stale bread
2 tablespoons butter or margarine

1. Trim crusts from bread. Cut bread into ½-inch cubes. Spread cubes on bottom of a shallow pan or baking sheet.
2. Bake at 350°F until golden but not browned.
3. Melt butter in a large skillet. Add toasted bread cubes. Stir-fry until all cubes are coated with butter. Cool and drain croutons on paper towels.

About ¾ cup

Cheese Croutons: Prepare croutons as directed. Mix **4 teaspoons grated Parmesan or Romano cheese** and **½ teaspoon paprika.** Toss hot croutons with cheese mixture.

Rice Noodles *(Kluski z Ryżu)*

1½ cups cooked rice
2 eggs
1 tablespoon butter or margarine
¼ teaspoon salt

1. Combine all ingredients. Beat until well mixed.
2. Drop by small spoonfuls into **boiling soup or broth.** Cook until noodles float, about 3 minutes.

About 2 cups

Chiffon Noodles *(Kluski z Piany)*

2 eggs, separated
2 tablespoons flour
¼ teaspoon salt

1. Beat egg whites and salt until stiff, not dry, peaks form.
2. Beat yolks separately just until frothy. Fold into whites. Fold in flour.
3. Gently spoon onto **boiling soup or broth.** Cover; cook 2 minutes. Turn; cook a few seconds longer.
4. To serve, break into separate portions with a spoon.

About 4 servings

Beaten Noodles *(Kluski Rozcierane)*

1 tablespoon butter or margarine
   (at room temperature)
2 whole eggs
2 egg yolks
3 tablespoons flour
¼ teaspoon salt

1. Beat butter until fluffy. Beat in whole eggs and egg yolks, one at a time. Mix in flour and salt.
2. Spoon into **boiling soup or bouillon.** Cover; cook 2 minutes. Turn. Cover and cook a few seconds longer.
3. To serve, break noodles into separate portions with a spoon.

About 6 servings

Egg Barley *(Zacierki)*

1 egg
3 tablespoons grated Parmesan
   cheese (optional)
   Dash salt
1 cup all-purpose flour (about)

1. Beat egg with cheese (if desired) and salt, then add flour until a thick dough forms.
2. On a floured surface, knead in more flour until a stiff, dry dough forms.
3. Grate dough onto waxed paper. Let dry 1 to 2 hours.
4. Cook in **boiling soup** about 5 minutes, or until egg barley floats.

About 1 cup dry; about 1¾ cups cooked

Egg Noodles *(Makaron)*

1 cup all-purpose flour
1 large egg
¼ teaspoon salt
½ eggshell of water (about 1
    tablespoon)

1. Mound flour on a board. Make a well in center; drop in egg and salt. Beat in water with a fork.
2. Knead from center to outer edges until dough is smooth.
3. Roll out very thin on a floured surface. Place sheet of dough on a cloth; let dry until not sticky but not too brittle to handle.
4. Sprinkle the sheet of noodle dough with flour. Roll up tightly and slice into thin threads. Toss the threads lightly to separate. Let dry 2 hours.
5. To cook, boil in **salted water** until the noodles rise to the top. Drain. Rinse in cold water. Drain again. Toss in **hot melted butter.**

About 2 cups uncooked

Egg Drops *(Kluski Lane)*

2 eggs, beaten
¼ teaspoon salt
1 tablespoon water
⅓ cup all-purpose flour

1. Combine all ingredients and stir until smooth.
2. Hold spoonfuls of batter about 12 inches from **boiling soup;** pour slowly from end of spoon. Let boil 2 to 3 minutes, until egg drops float.

About 4 servings

String Dumplings: Prepare Egg Drops batter. Pour almost continuously from a cup or spoon into boiling soup to form long "strings." Break apart after cooking.

Potato Dumplings *(Kartoflane Kluski)*

2 cups hot mashed potatoes
⅓ cup fine dry bread crumbs
2 egg yolks
¾ teaspoon salt
¼ teaspoon pepper
⅓ cup all-purpose flour
2 egg whites, beaten until stiff, but
    not dry

1. Mix ingredients in a large bowl in the order given.
2. Place on floured board and roll to pencil thickness. Cut into 2- or 3-inch strips.
3. Drop into **boiling salted water.** Cook until dumplings float to top.

Croquettes: Sauté ½ **cup chopped onion** in **2 tablespoons butter.** Proceed as in recipe for Potato Dumplings; add onion to potatoes. Roll strips in **fine dry bread crumbs.** Pan-fry in **butter** until golden brown.

Suet or Marrow Balls *(Pulpety z Łoju lub Szpiku)*

½ pound white beef suet from
    kidneys, or marrow
2 eggs, slightly beaten
½ teaspoon salt
¼ teaspoon pepper
½ cup fine dry bread crumbs or
    cracker meal
2 teaspoons chopped fresh dill or
    parsley
Flour
Broth or desired soup

1. Remove membrane from suet or marrow. Chop fine and put into a bowl.
2. Add eggs, salt, pepper, bread crumbs, and dill to suet; mix thoroughly but lightly. Form into small round balls.
3. Roll in flour and drop into gently boiling broth or soup. Cook 10 minutes, or until balls float.

About 2½ dozen balls

Egg Balls *(Kluski z Żółtek)*

4 hard-cooked egg yolks
4 raw egg yolks
¼ teaspoon salt
⅛ teaspoon nutmeg
⅛ teaspoon pepper

1. Mash the cooked egg yolks or press through a sieve. Add raw yolks and seasonings. Mix until a smooth thick paste forms.
2. Drop by spoonfuls into **boiling soup or broth.** Cook a few seconds until egg balls float. Serve immediately.

4 to 6 servings

Fish Dumplings *(Pulpety z Ryby)*

1 onion, minced
1 tablespoon butter or margarine
1 pound cooked fish or 2 cups flaked cooked fish
1 slice white bread, soaked in water and squeezed
2 eggs
¾ teaspoon salt
2 tablespoons fine dry bread crumbs
1 teaspoon dill weed
1 teaspoon chopped parsley
2 tablespoons flour

1. Fry onion in butter until golden.
2. Flake or chop fish very fine. Or, grind fish with the onion.
3. Mix fish with bread and eggs. Season with salt and pepper. Stir in bread crumbs, dill, and parsley.
4. Form balls about 1½ inches in diameter. Roll in flour.
5. Cook in **boiling water** until dumplings float, about 4 minutes.

4 to 6 servings

Liver Mounds *(Babki z Wątróbek)*

¾ pound chicken, turkey, or capon livers
1 cup milk
1 tablespoon butter or margarine
⅓ cup minced onion
⅓ cup fine dry bread crumbs
3 eggs, separated
½ teaspoon salt

1. Soak livers in milk in a glass or pottery bowl 3 hours in refrigerator. Drain livers, discarding milk. Mince livers.
2. Melt butter in a skillet. Add onion and stir-fry until golden. Remove from heat.
3. Combine minced liver, onion with butter, bread crumbs, and egg yolks. Mix until thoroughly combined.
4. Beat egg whites with salt until stiff, not dry, peaks are formed. Fold into liver mixture.
5. Spoon liver mixture into well-greased muffin-pan wells. Grease a piece of brown paper or waxed paper on one side. Place paper, greased side down, on top of muffin pan.
6. Bake at 350°F 25 to 35 minutes. Remove at once from pan. Serve hot with **a piquant sauce** or in **chicken broth.**

About 6 servings

Raw Potato Dumplings *(Kartoflane Kluski)*

2 cups grated raw potatoes
2 eggs
1 teaspoon salt
½ cup fine dry bread crumbs
1½ cups all-purpose flour (about)
Boiling salted water

1. Rinse potatoes in cold water; drain well.
2. Combine potatoes in a large bowl with eggs, salt, crumbs, and enough flour to make a stiff dough.
3. Using a wet spoon, drop tablespoonfuls of dough into boiling salted water.
4. Cook until dumplings float to the top. Dumplings should be about 1½ × ½ inches when done.

About 6 servings

Take the chill out of a winter's day by serving the hearty **Polish Noodles and Cabbage, 58,** topped, for zest, with caraway seed.

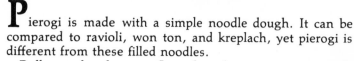

Pierogi is made with a simple noodle dough. It can be compared to ravioli, won ton, and kreplach, yet pierogi is different from these filled noodles.

Roll out dough on a floured surface to ⅛- or ¼-inch thickness. Cut out circles of dough, about 4 inches in diameter, from the dough. Place a rounded tablespoon of filling to one side of each circle, then fold the dough over to make a half moon. Carefully seal edges by pinching together or crimping with the tines of a fork. Filling varies from mashed potatoes to fruit; meat and sauerkraut are popular and cheese fillings may be sweet or savory.

Typical Polish pierogi are cooked in boiling salted water. Use at least 2 quarts of water and 1 teaspoon salt in a kettle. Add only enough pierogi to the boiling water to make one layer. Crowding makes pierogi stick together and become misshapen or lumpy. Count cooking time after the water returns to boiling. About 4 to 6 minutes in boiling water lightens pierogi and makes them float. Then the pierogi are done.

Remove cooked pierogi with a perforated spoon. Serve plain or drizzle with melted butter. To serve Polish style, sprinkle pierogi with buttered bread crumbs (add **¼ cup dry bread crumbs** to **2 tablespoons melted butter**; stir in **¼ teaspoon salt** and **⅛ teaspoon pepper**).

Yeast pierogi is made with a rich yeast dough. The shape is somewhat like Parker House rolls, but with a meat or cheese or sauerkraut filling. Both Russia and Latvia take credit for introducing yeast pierogi into Poland—and for kulebiak as well.

Roll out the raised dough to ⅜-inch thickness on floured surface. Cut out 3-inch circles. Place a rounded tablespoon of filling to one side of each circle. Fold other side of dough over filling. Pinch edges to seal. Place about 1½ inches apart on greased baking sheet. Bake at 350°F about 20 to 35 minutes.

Yeast pierogi are served as appetizers at parties or soup accompaniments for Polish family meals.

Uszka, which means "little ears" in Polish, is a small filled noodle similar to the tortellini ("little hats") of Italy. Favorite fillings for the Polish uszka are mushroom or meat.

Roll out dough on a floured surface to about ⅛-inch thickness. Cut into 2- or 3-inch squares. Place a rounded teaspoon of filling toward one corner of each square. Fold opposite corner of dough over filling to make a triangle. Seal edges by pinching or crimping with tines of a fork. Then make a circle by bringing the two long narrow corners together; seal. Set the uszka, circle side down, so the wide triangle stands up. This allows the filled noodles to dry slightly while remainder are filled and shaped.

Cook uszka in boiling salted water or boiling broth, a few at a time. Count cooking time of about 5 minutes from water's return to boiling. Uszka are done when they float. Remove with perforated spoon; keep warm until all are

This exquisite setting of Polish china and crystal highlights **Ham in Rye Crust, 78, Roast Turkey, 55,** and **Potato Dumplings, 31.**

cooked. Serve in broth or in soup. Or serve with a topping of buttered bread crumbs.

Kolduny is a stuffed noodle which came to Poland from Lithuania. These noodles are very small circles of dough, usually filled with lamb or beef.

Roll out half of dough for pierogi or uszka on floured surface to ⅛-inch thickness. Dot with teaspoonfuls of filling, about 2 inches apart. Roll out remaining dough on floured surface. Carefully place second sheet of dough on top of mounds of filling; adjust loosely. With a small glass (1 to 1½ inches in diameter) dipped in flour, cut out circles of dough, each with a mound of filling in the center. Seal edges by pinching.

Cook kolduny in boiling broth or soup until they float, about 3 minutes. Serve in soup.

Naleśniki is the Polish name for pancakes. Thick pancakes and thin pancakes, with all the variations between, are part of Polish cuisine.

Thin pancakes, like crepes, are best for drier fillings similar to those used for the filled noodles. The sides can be folded over the filling while rolling up the pancake; this makes a neat package. Then further cooking is usually done. Thick pancakes usually are just rolled up with the filling and served without further cooking.

Pour thin pancake batter into skillet which is well-oiled but has no excess oil visible. Use about 2 tablespoons batter for each pancake in an 8-inch skillet. Tilt skillet while pouring batter to spread batter evenly over skillet. Cook over medium heat until dry on the edges; flip pancake and cook other side until golden. Remove to a plate. Wipe skillet with oil-soaked cloth after each pancake. Thin pancakes can be prepared ahead of time and filled. Keep in refrigerator. Then finish cooking just before serving.

Pour thick pancake batter into a well-oiled skillet. Use about ⅓ cup batter for each 6-inch pancake. Cook until edges are no longer shiny and no more bubbles appear on top. Turn pancake; cook second side until golden. Fill and serve thick pancakes at once.

To fill pancakes, place a heaping spoonful of filling near one edge. Roll pancake over filling. Place seam-side down on plate. Keep sides of thin pancakes tucked in, over filling, while rolling. Spinach, mushrooms, brains, and cheese are favorite fillings.

To finish filled thin pancakes, sauté in butter in skillet until crisp on all sides. Or dip in beaten egg, then coat with fine dry bread crumbs. Fry in hot oil or butter until golden brown on all sides.

Kulebiak translates as "fingers." This filled yeast bread is sometimes made in time-saving form as a long roll. Then the crusty slices are served as individual portions.

Proofing (rising) is done after the kneaded dough has been shaped or rolled out and filled. For appetizers and soup accompaniments, sometimes only a sprinkle of caraway seed is used with plain kulebiak. But fillings are often used when kulebiak are served for parties or as a main dish for family suppers in Polish homes.

Fillings are usually meat or vegetables, with mushrooms a traditional holiday favorite.

Knead dough until it forms a smooth ball. Form plain kulebiak into thin rolls about 5 inches long. For filled kulebiak, roll out dough on floured surface to form an 18×6-inch rectangle.

To make a roll for slicing, spoon filling lengthwise down center of dough. Fold dough to center, over filling. Pinch to seal all edges and place, seam side down, on greased baking sheet. Cover with plastic wrap and let rise for 30 minutes. Make ½-inch deep slashes in top, about 1 inch apart. Brush with beaten egg, if desired. Bake at 375°F about 1 hour, or until golden brown. Slice when cooled.

For individual kulebiak without filling, place the 5-inch rolls on greased baking sheet. Cover with plastic wrap and let rise 30 minutes. Brush with **beaten egg** and sprinkle with **caraway seed.** Then bake at 375°F about 15 minutes, or until golden.

For individual kulebiak with filling, roll out each 5-inch piece of dough on a floured surface to form small rectangles. Place 1 tablespoon filling on each rectangle. Bring edges of dough lengthwise to center and pinch together to seal. Place on greased baking sheet. Cover with plastic wrap and let rise 30 minutes. Brush with beaten egg. Bake at 375°F about 20 to 35 minutes or until golden brown.

Serve kulebiak warm or cooled.

Yeast Pierogi *(Pierożki)*

4 eggs
1 tablespoon melted butter
1 teaspoon salt
1 package active dry yeast
¼ cup warm water
1 cup dairy sour cream
1 tablespoon sugar
1½ teaspoons grated lemon peel (optional)
4 cups all-purpose flour (about)
Filling (see pages 38–40)

1. Beat eggs with melted butter and salt until thick and fluffy.
2. Dissolve yeast in warm water in a large bowl. Let stand 10 minutes.
3. Add egg mixture to yeast. Beat in sour cream, sugar, and, if desired, lemon peel. Stir in flour, 1 cup at a time, until dough is firm but not stiff.
4. Turn dough on floured surface; knead 3 minutes. Place dough in a greased bowl. Cover with plastic wrap. Let rise in a warm place until doubled, about 1 hour.
5. Roll out dough to ⅜-inch thickness on floured surface. Cut into 3-inch rounds.
6. Place a spoonful of filling a little to one side of each round. Moisten edges. Fold over and seal. Place on greased baking sheet.
7. Bake at 350°F about 20 to 35 minutes, or until golden brown.

About 3 dozen

Pierogi

2 cups all-purpose flour
2 eggs
½ teaspoon salt
⅓ cup water
Filling (see pages 38–40)

1. Mound flour on a bread board and make a well in the center.
2. Drop eggs and salt into well. Add water; working from the center to outside of flour mound, mix flour into liquid in center with one hand and keep flour mounded with other hand. Knead until dough is firm and well mixed.
3. Cover dough with a warm bowl; let rest 10 minutes.
4. Divide dough into halves. On floured surface, using half of dough at a time, roll dough as thin as possible.
5. Cut out 3-inch rounds with large biscuit cutter.
6. Place a small spoonful of filling a little to one side on each round of dough. Moisten edge with water, fold over and press edges together firmly. Be sure they are well sealed to prevent the filling from leaking out.
7. Drop pierogi into **boiling salted water.** Cook gently 3 to 5 minutes, or until pierogi float. Lift out of water with perforated spoon.

1½ to 2 dozen

Note: The dough will have a tendency to dry. A dry dough will not seal completely. Work with half the dough at a time, rolling out a large circle of dough and placing small mounds of filling far enough apart to allow for cutting. Then cut with biscuit cutter and seal firmly.

Never put too many pierogi in cooking water. The uncooked will stick together and the cooked get lumpy and tough.

Little Ears (Uszka)

2 cups all-purpose flour
½ cup water
1 egg
⅛ teaspoon salt
Filling (see pages 38–40)

1. Mound flour on a bread board and make a well in the center. Place remaining ingredients in the well. Mix flour into liquid in center until a dough is formed. Knead thoroughly.
2. Roll dough very thinly on a floured surface. Cut into 2-inch squares.
3. Put a spoonful of filling in center of each square. Fold so that the corners meet in the middle. Press together with fingers to seal. Fold in half diagonally, so the square becomes a triangle. Seal edges. Then bring the 2 long ends of triangle together; press firmly to seal.
4. Drop into **boiling soup.** Cook until the uszka float.

About 3 dozen

Thin Pancakes (Naleśniki)

½ cup all-purpose flour
1 egg
1 egg yolk
½ cup milk
1 teaspoon sugar
⅛ teaspoon salt

1. Combine flour, egg, and egg yolk in a small bowl of electric mixer. Beat just to mix. Add milk, sugar, and salt; beat at low speed 2 minutes.
2. Heat a small, heavy skillet. Brush bottom with oil.
3. Pour about 2 tablespoons batter into skillet; at once tilt skillet to spread batter evenly over bottom of skillet. When

Salad oil
Filling (see pages 38–40)

edges are dry, turn pancake and cook other side.

4. Repeat until all batter is used, reserve some batter for coating stuffed pancakes, if desired.

5. For stuffed pancakes, place 1 heaping tablespoonful of filling in center of pancake. Fold sides toward center, over filling, and roll up pancakes.

6. Dip in **egg** beaten with **water** or in reserved batter. Coat with **fine dry bread crumbs.**

7. Quickly fry coated pancakes in a small amount of hot oil. Turn and cook until golden on all sides.

12 pancakes

Thick Pancakes *(Naleśniki)*

1 cup milk
1 egg
1 cup all-purpose flour
⅓ cup water
¼ teaspoon salt
Salad oil or melted butter
Filling (see pages 38–40)

1. Beat milk and egg until frothy. Add flour and beat rapidly 1 minute. Add water and salt. Beat rapidly 1 minute longer.

2. Heat a small, heavy skillet. Brush bottom with oil or wipe with cloth dipped in oil. (Do not use too much oil.)

3. Pour about 2 tablespoons batter onto bottom of skillet; at once tilt skillet so batter spreads evenly. When edge of pancake begins to dry, turn and cook other side.

4. Repeat until all the batter is used.

12 pancakes

Yeast Fingers *(Drożdżowe Paluszki)*

2 cups all-purpose flour
1 package active dry yeast
1 teaspoon sugar
½ teaspoon salt
½ cup butter or margarine
1 egg
2 egg yolks
2 tablespoons dairy sour cream
1 egg white
2 tablespoons caraway seed or
    poppy seed

1. Combine flour, yeast, sugar, and salt in a bowl. Cut in butter with a pastry blender or two knives until well mixed. Stir in egg, egg yolks, and sour cream.

2. Knead the dough in the bowl a few minutes until it forms a smooth ball.

3. Break off small bits of dough, about 1 tablespoonful each; roll between palms of hands to form long, thin rolls.

4. Place on a greased baking sheet. Let rise in a warm place until doubled in bulk.

5. Brush with egg white, then sprinkle with caraway seed.

6. Bake at 375°F 15 minutes, or until golden. Remove immediately from the baking sheet.

About 40 fingers

Stuffed Yeast Fingers: Two ways are typical, either a long roll which is sliced after baking, or individual fingers.

For long roll, roll out the dough on a floured surface to form a rectangle about 18×6 inches. Spoon filling lengthwise down center of dough. Fold over both long sides and seal the top seam and ends. Carefully place, seam-side down, on a greased baking sheet. Cover with plastic wrap. Let rise in a warm place 30 minutes. Brush top with slightly beaten **egg white.** Cut ½-inch deep slashes across top, about 1 inch apart. Bake at 375°F 1 hour. Cool 15 minutes before slicing.

For individual fingers, roll out dough as directed. Cut into 48 pieces and roll each piece into a rectangle. Place 1 tablespoon filling on each rectangle. Fold dough lengthwise over filling and pinch to seal all seams. Place on greased baking sheet. Cover; let rise, and brush with egg white as directed. Do not slash. Bake at 375°F about 20 to 35 minutes, or until golden brown.

Beef Filling

1 large onion, halved and sliced
2 tablespoons margarine or
   shortening
1¾ cups ground cooked beef
¾ cup cooked rice
2 teaspoons instant bouillon or
   meat extract
3 tablespoons hot water
1 tablespoon chopped fresh
   parsley
   Salt and pepper

1. Stir-fry onion in margarine in a large skillet until golden. Stir in meat and rice.
2. Dissolve bouillon in hot water. Add to meat mixture with parsley and salt and pepper to taste.

About 2½ cups

Cooked Meat Filling

2 onions, minced
2 tablespoons butter or margarine
1 cup ground cooked meat
2 slices stale white bread
   Milk or water
½ teaspoon salt
¼ teaspoon pepper

1. Stir-fry onion in butter in a heavy skillet 5 minutes. Add ground meat. Remove from heat.
2. Soak bread in just enough milk to cover. When thoroughly soaked, about 10 minutes, squeeze out excess milk.
3. Stir bread, salt, and pepper into onion mixture until well combined.

2 to 3 cups

Meat Filling

¼ pound suet, chopped
2 cups grated onion
½ pound ground lean beef
½ pound ground lean lamb
½ pound ground lean veal
1 teaspoon salt
¾ teaspoon marjoram
¾ teaspoon sweet basil
¼ teaspoon pepper
⅓ cup fine dry bread crumbs
   Meat stock

1. Fry suet and onion just until onion is tender. Add meat; fry until meat changes color.
2. Stir in all seasonings and bread crumbs. Add just enough meat stock to make a paste.

About 3½ cups

Sausage Filling

10 ounces Polish sausage (kiełbasa),
   skinned and chopped
½ cup grated cheese or chopped
   mushrooms
¼ cup fine dry bread crumbs
1 egg

Combine all ingredients thoroughly.

About 2 cups

Brains Filling

1 pair fresh veal or pork brains
　(about 12 ounces)
　Water
1 teaspoon salt
5 peppercorns
1 bay leaf
1 tablespoon vinegar
⅓ cup finely chopped onion
3 tablespoons butter
1 egg yolk
　Salt and pepper

1. Rinse brains under running cold water.
2. Put brains into a saucepan with water to cover, 1 teaspoon salt, peppercorns, bay leaf, and vinegar. Bring to boiling and cook 3 minutes.
3. Drain brains; remove and discard white tough membrane. Chop brains coarsely.
4. Sauté onion in butter until golden. Add the brains and stir to mix well. Cook 2 minutes. Add egg yolk to mixture and blend well. Season to taste with salt and pepper.

About 1 cup

Mushroom Filling

1½ cups chopped mushrooms
½ cup chopped onion
2 tablespoons butter or margarine
¼ teaspoon salt
⅛ teaspoon pepper
2 egg yolks or 1 egg, beaten

1. Stir-fry mushrooms and onion in butter until onion is soft. Remove from heat.
2. Stir in remaining ingredients.

About 1 cup

Cabbage and Mushroom Filling with Egg

1 small head cabbage (about 1
　pound) shredded
⅓ cup water
1 large onion, halved and sliced
1 can (4 ounces) mushroom stems
　and pieces
2 tablespoons butter or margarine
1 teaspoon salt
¼ teaspoon pepper
2 hard-cooked eggs, chopped

1. Combine the cabbage, water, onion, mushrooms, and butter in a large saucepan. Cook, covered, over low heat until tender, about 30 minutes.
2. Add salt, pepper, and chopped eggs; mix well.

About 3½ cups

Sauerkraut Filling

⅓ cup chopped onion
1 tablespoon butter or margarine
1½ cups finely chopped sauerkraut
2 tablespoons dairy sour cream

1. Stir-fry onion in butter in a saucepan 3 minutes.
2. Rinse and drain sauerkraut. Add to onion and cook 2 minutes.
3. Remove from heat. Stir in sour cream.

About 1½ cups

Potato Filling

½ cup chopped onion
2 tablespoons butter
½ teaspoon salt
¼ teaspoon white pepper
2 cups mashed potatoes

1. Sauté onion in butter 5 minutes. Stir in salt and pepper.
2. Combine potatoes and onion mixture. Blend well.

About 2 cups

Sauerkraut and Mushroom Filling

2½ cups sauerkraut
  Boiling water
2 tablespoons fat
½ cup chopped onion
4 ounces mushrooms, sliced
¼ teaspoon salt
¼ teaspoon pepper
1 hard-cooked egg, chopped
2 tablespoons dairy sour cream

1. Rinse sauerkraut and drain. Put into a saucepan. Cover with a small amount of boiling water. Cook 20 minutes; drain.
2. Heat fat in a skillet. Add onion and fry until golden. Add mushrooms and fry 3 minutes. Stir in sauerkraut, salt, and pepper. Fry until the sauerkraut becomes golden, about 20 minutes.
3. Remove from heat. Add chopped egg and sour cream; mix well.

About 2 cups

Savory Cheese Filling

1½ cups pot cheese or farmer cheese
1 teaspoon lemon juice
1 teaspoon sugar
1 egg
1 egg yolk
¼ teaspoon salt

Press cheese through a sieve into a bowl. Add remaining ingredients; mix well.

About 1½ cups

Sweet Cheese Filling

1½ cups pot cheese, farmer cheese, or ricotta
1 egg, beaten
3 tablespoons sugar
¼ cup raisins or currants
½ teaspoon vanilla extract
¼ teaspoon cinnamon

Press cheese through a sieve into a bowl. Add remaining ingredients; mix well.

About 1¾ cups

Cooked Fruit Filling

2 cups pitted cherries, apples, or blueberries
¾ cup water
⅓ cup sugar (optional)
½ teaspoon cinnamon or cardamom (optional)
1 teaspoon lemon juice (optional)
2 to 4 tablespoons fine dry bread crumbs

1. Combine fruit, water, and sugar in a saucepan. Bring to boiling; cook and stir until fruit is tender and water is almost gone. Remove from heat.
2. Mash fruit slightly with potato masher. Add cinnamon and lemon juice. Cook and stir over low heat just until fruit mixture is thick.
3. Stir in enough bread crumbs to make filling very thick.

About 1½ cups

Prune Filling

2 cups dried prunes
1 tablespoon lemon juice
1 tablespoon brown sugar

1. Cover prunes with **water.** Bring just to boiling. Cover. Remove from heat and let stand 20 minutes. Remove and discard pits.
2. Add lemon juice and sugar. Cook until almost all liquid is gone.

About 1½ cups

ENTRÉES

The search for new ways to prepare chicken is eternal. It is the one economical meat that everyone seems to like—but not always done in the same fashion. Polish cuisine offers some very original tastes. Capon in Cream is exceptional. You will also want to try fish done with a Polish flair and, for real down-home Polish cooking, don't miss the three cabbage-roll recipes.

Hussar Roast (Pieczeń Huzarska)

⅔ cup vinegar or vodka
1 beef round rump roast, boneless, or round tip roast (3 pounds)
1 cup all-purpose flour
1 teaspoon salt
¼ teaspoon pepper
¼ cup butter, melted
1 large onion, quartered
1 cup bouillon or meat stock

Stuffing:
1 tablespoon butter
2 medium onions, minced
¼ cup fine dry bread crumbs
1 egg, beaten

1. Heat vinegar just to boiling in a large casserole or skillet. Add meat, turning to scald all sides. Drain meat. Discard vinegar.
2. Mix flour, salt, and pepper. Coat meat with seasoned flour. Reserve 2 tablespoons seasoned flour.
3. Brown meat in butter in a Dutch oven or heavy skillet. Add quartered onion and bouillon. Cover; simmer 2 hours, or until meat is tender.
4. Slice meat about 1 inch thick. Then slit each slice, making a pocket.
5. For stuffing, melt butter. Sauté minced onion until transparent. Stir in bread crumbs and 1 tablespoon seasoned flour. Remove from heat. Stir in egg.
6. Stuff crumb mixture into pockets in meat. Close and skewer with wooden picks. Tie together with string in original roast shape. Return to Dutch oven. Sprinkle with remaining tablespoon seasoned flour. Cover; cook over medium-low heat 30 minutes.

About 8 servings

Beef Pot Roast (*Pieczeń Wołowa Duszona*)

1 beef round rump or chuck roast,
    boneless (3½ pounds)
3 tablespoons salad oil or ¼
    pound salt pork, diced
    Bouillon or meat broth (about 1½
    cups)
1 bay leaf
2 onions, quartered
2 carrots, cut in pieces
½ teaspoon salt
½ teaspoon coarse pepper
    Flour
    Salt and pepper

1. Brown the beef in oil. Add ¼ cup bouillon, bay leaf, onions, carrots, salt, and pepper; cover and simmer 2½ hours, basting with additional bouillon to prevent burning.
2. Sprinkle flour over meat and turn it over. Sprinkle with more flour. If necessary, add more bouillon for the sauce. Cook uncovered 30 minutes. Serve the pot roast with **noodles** or **potatoes** and any kind of vegetables.

8 to 10 servings

Pot Roast with Sour Cream: Prepare Beef Pot Roast as directed. Add **1½ cups dairy sour cream** instead of bouillon after flouring the meat. Finish cooking as directed.

Pot Roast with Sour Cream and Pickles or Mushrooms: Prepare Beef Pot Roast as directed. Add **1½ cups dairy sour cream** instead of bouillon after flouring the meat. Then stir in **⅔ cup chopped dill pickles** or **1 cup sliced mushrooms**. Finish cooking as directed.

Beef Slices with Sour Cream and Mushrooms (*Zrazy z Grzybami i ze Śmietaną*)

½ cup all-purpose flour
1 teaspoon salt
½ teaspoon pepper
2 pounds beef eye round, top
    round, or sirloin (cut in thin
    steaks)
3 tablespoons butter or fat
1 can (4 ounces) mushrooms with
    liquid
1 cup water
6 medium potatoes, cooked; or 3
    cups sauerkraut, drained
1 tablespoon flour
1 cup dairy sour cream

1. Mix flour with salt and pepper. Coat meat with seasoned flour.
2. Melt butter in a large skillet or Dutch oven. Brown meat quickly on both sides.
3. Add mushrooms with liquid and water. Cover. Simmer 1 hour, basting occasionally with sauce.
4. Add potatoes to meat; cook 10 minutes, or until meat and potatoes are tender.
5. Blend flour into sour cream. Blend into sauce. Bring to boiling, then simmer 5 minutes.

6 servings

Steamed Beef (*Sztuka Mięsa w Parze*)

3 to 4 pounds beef round rump or
    eye round steak
    Salt and pepper
2 onions, sliced
1 cup each diced carrot, parsley
    root, and parsnips
1 cup green peas
½ cup sliced celery
½ cup asparagus stems (optional)
1 cauliflower or cabbage core, diced
    (optional)
2 tablespoons butter

1. Pound the meat. Sprinkle with salt and pepper. Let stand 30 minutes. Pound again.
2. In a steamer top, combine meat and vegetables. Add butter. Cook over gently boiling water about 3 hours, or until meat is tender.
3. Slice·meat. Serve with the steamed vegetables, boiled potatoes, and Horseradish Sauce (page 88), if desired.

6 to 8 servings

Fish is an important part of the Polish diet. More care is taken in its preparation, it seems, than in beef preparation. Always the flavor should be delicate, the texture tender and flaky.

POACHING

Place **fish,** whole or cut into serving pieces, directly in bottom of pan, adding (per pound):

- **1 tablespoon butter**
- **½ cup fish stock or chicken broth**
- **3 tablespoons white wine**
- **¼ teaspoon salt**
  Dash pepper

Cover tightly and simmer slowly. Note that only a small amount of liquid is used. Poach about 10 minutes per pound of fish, or about 5 to 6 minutes per inch of thickness.

BOILING

Fish may be cooked whole or cut into serving pieces. A large fish looks best served whole when appearance counts. For easiest handling, cooking should be done in a large oblong pan on a rack (a roasting pan with cover can double for a fish kettle); for additional ease, the fish may be wrapped in cheesecloth.

- **1 quart water**
- **1 large onion, quartered**
- **2 carrots, cut in half**
- **½ celery root**
- **½ parsley root or 2 sprigs parsley**
- **2 celery stalks with leaves, cut in half**
- **1 thick slice of lemon**
- **½ bay leaf (optional)**
  Salt, pepper, thyme, oregano, tarragon, peppercorns

1. Combine water, vegetables, and seasonings to taste. Cook until vegetables are tender. Strain.
2. Wrap **fish** in cheesecloth and place on rack, belly down, in fish kettle. Add enough of the strained liquid to cover. Simmer until fish flakes easily, about 5 minutes per inch of thickness, or about 10 minutes per pound. Remove fish on rack and drain; cut cheesecloth and remove carefully.
3. The stock may be used as the basis of a fish chowder or for other recipes. Vegetables may be used for garnish. Note that enough liquid is used to completely cover the fish.

STEAMING

Place **fish,** whole or cut into serving pieces, on rack over enough **fish stock** or **water** to allow plenty of steam throughout cooking time. Cover very tightly. Simmer; do not boil. Steam about 12 minutes per pound of fish or 5 minutes per inch of thickness. Remove fish.

FRYING

Small fish may be fried whole, with or without the heads, according to preference. Cut large fish into chunks, steaks,

or fillets for frying. Wash and drain the **fish.** Coat with **flour** seasoned with **salt** and **pepper.** (For each ½ cup flour, use ½ teaspoon salt and ⅛ teaspoon pepper.) Fry either in deep fat at 350°F or in a small amount of oil or butter in a skillet. Use **butter, olive oil,** or **vegetable oil** according to personal taste. Fish may also be fried without being coated with flour. Another method is to dip fish in **beaten egg** and then coat with **seasoned dry bread crumbs.** In all cases frying should be done over medium heat. Fish should be turned carefully only once. Fry until a light, golden brown.

BROILING

Brush **whole fish** or **pieces** with **melted butter** or **other fat.** Preheat broiler about 10 minutes; brush with oil just before placing fish on rack. It is important to preheat the broiler for best results. A special wire basket for whole fish is available. It is especially useful for broiling or grilling on an outdoor barbecue. Baste fish frequently. Larger fish should be split for broiling and placed skin-side down. Broil for 5 to 10 minutes on each side, or until fish flakes easily.

BAKING

Arrange **whole fish** or **pieces** close together in a well-buttered shallow pan or casserole. Spoon **melted butter** or a **sauce** over fish. Bake at 350°F about 20 minutes per inch of thickness, or 15 to 20 minutes per pound. Often **lemon juice** and **chopped parsley** are sprinkled on top of fish during the last minutes of baking. Fish fillets may also be coated with **seasoned flour** or **bread crumbs** as in frying; sauté quickly before baking.

Baked Leftover Fish *(Potrawa Zapiekana)*

  3 **boiled potatoes, sliced**
1½ **cups diced cooked fish**
  ¾ **cup sliced cooked cauliflower or**
      mushrooms (optional)
  2 **hard-cooked eggs, sliced**
    Salt and pepper
  1 **tablespoon flour**
  1 **cup dairy sour cream**
  ¼ **cup water**
  3 **tablespoons bread crumbs**
  2 **tablespoons grated Parmesan**
      cheese
  2 **tablespoons butter**

1. Arrange layers of half the potatoes, fish, cauliflower, eggs, and remaining potatoes in a greased 1½-quart casserole. Lightly sprinkle salt and pepper over each layer.
2. Blend flour into sour cream; stir in water. Spoon over casserole mixture.
3. Mix bread crumbs, cheese, and butter together. Sprinkle over top of casserole.
4. Bake at 350°F 30 minutes.

About 4 servings

Sole with Vegetables *(Sola z Jarzynami)*

  2 **tablespoons butter or margarine**
  1 **large onion, diced**
  1 **cup savoy cabbage, shredded**
      (optional)
  1 **leek, thinly sliced**

1. Melt butter in a Dutch oven or large skillet. Add vegetables and stir-fry 5 minutes.
2. Sprinkle fish fillets with salt. Place on the vegetables. Add water. Cover; simmer 15 minutes.
3. For sauce, melt butter in a saucepan. Stir in flour. Cook

1 large carrot, thinly sliced
1 stalk celery, thinly sliced
1 parsley root, thinly sliced
2 pounds sole or any white fish
    fillets
½ teaspoon salt
2 tablespoons water
Sauce:
    2 tablespoons butter or margarine
    2 tablespoons flour
    1 cup chicken broth or fish stock
    ½ teaspoon salt
    ¼ teaspoon pepper
    ¼ cup dairy sour cream

and stir until golden. Then gradually stir in broth. Cook, stirring constantly, until sauce boils.

4. Transfer the fish to a warm platter. Stir the sauce into the vegetables. Remove from heat. Season with salt and pepper; stir in sour cream. Pour over the fish.

About 6 servings

Fish au Gratin *(Ryba Zapiekana)*

1 cup chicken or vegetable broth
    or stock
1 tablespoon flour
1 tablespoon butter or margarine
    (at room temperature)
½ teaspoon salt
¼ teaspoon parsley flakes
¼ teaspoon pepper
    Pinch ground thyme
¼ cup whipping cream
1½ pounds sole, trout, pike, or
    other white fish
3 tablespoons grated Parmesan,
    Swiss, or Gruyère cheese
2 tablespoons dry bread crumbs
1 tablespoon melted butter or
    margarine
1 teaspoon lemon juice (optional)

1. Bring broth to boiling in a small saucepan. Blend flour into butter and stir into boiling broth. Cook and stir until thickened. Reduce heat. Stir in salt, parsley flakes, pepper, thyme, and cream.
2. Place fish in a well-buttered pan. Pour sauce over fish.
3. Bake at 375°F 15 minutes.
4. Mix cheese, bread crumbs, melted butter, and lemon juice (if desired). Sprinkle over fish in pan. Bake about 15 minutes longer, or until fish flakes easily.

4 to 6 servings

Fish au Gratin with Tomatoes: Prepare Fish au Gratin as directed, except sprinkle **½ cup chopped tomato** over top of fish before covering with sauce.

Fish au Gratin with Mushrooms: Prepare Fish au Gratin as directed, adding **½ cup sliced mushrooms** to partially baked fish before topping with crumb mixture.

Fish au Gratin with Horseradish: Prepare Fish au Gratin as directed, adding **4 teaspoons prepared horseradish** to sauce along with cream.

Roulade of Eel *(Rolada z Węgorza)*

1 eel (2 pounds)
3 hard-cooked eggs, chopped
2 dill pickles, chopped
4 mushrooms, sliced
1 egg
1 teaspoon salt
¼ teaspoon pepper
1 quart vegetable stock or
    consommé
⅓ cup vinegar

1. Skin eel. Split in half; remove bones. Lay half the eel on a double thickness of cheesecloth.
2. Mix hard-cooked eggs, pickles, mushrooms, raw egg, salt, and pepper. Spread over the eel on cloth. Top with other half of eel. Wrap eel in the cloth. Place in a large kettle.
3. Add stock and vinegar to kettle. Boil gently 30 minutes. Let cool 1½ hours.
4. To serve, remove eel from cloth. Set on platter. Garnish, if desired. Serve with a sauce such as Mustard Sauce (page 63) or Horseradish Sauce (page 88).

About 6 servings

Northern Pike Polish Style
(Szczupak po Polsku)

1 dressed northern pike, perch, or
    other white fish (2 pounds)
1 carrot
1 onion
1 stalk celery
10 peppercorns
1½ teaspoons salt
    Water
Topping:
  ¼ cup butter
  6 hard-cooked eggs, finely
     chopped
  ¼ cup lemon juice
  1 tablespoon chopped fresh dill or
     parsley
  ¾ teaspoon salt
  ¼ teaspoon pepper

1. Put fish into a large kettle. Add carrot, onion, celery, peppercorns, and salt. Add enough water to cover. Cover; boil gently about 15 to 20 minutes, or until fish flakes easily.
2. Meanwhile, heat butter in a skillet. Add chopped eggs, lemon juice, dill, salt, and pepper. Cook 5 minutes, stirring frequently.
3. When fish is cooked, set it on a warm platter. Spoon topping over fish. Serve with boiled potatoes, if desired.

4 to 6 servings

Pike or Carp Stuffed with Anchovies
(Szczupak lub Karp Nadziewany Sardelami)

1 can (2 ounces) flat anchovy fillets
1 pike (3 pounds) with milt and
    liver, or other white fish
¼ cup butter or margarine (at room
    temperature)
2 eggs, separated
½ cup grated fresh bread
¼ cup melted butter for basting
1 cup dairy sour cream

1. Cut half the anchovies in thin strips. Lard the fish with strips of anchovy.
2. Chop or mash remaining anchovies; cream with 2 tablespoons of butter. Divide in half.
3. For stuffing, beat egg yolks. Chop liver. Combine grated bread, egg yolks, milt, and liver. Add half of anchovy butter; mix well. Beat egg whites until stiff peaks are formed; fold into bread mixture.
4. Fill cavity of fish with stuffing. Close cavity with skewers or wooden picks. Place fish in roasting pan. Drizzle with half the melted butter.
5. Bake at 350°F 30 minutes. Baste with remaining melted butter. Bake 10 minutes longer. Spread remaining anchovy butter over fish. Top with sour cream. Continue baking until fish is tender and flakes easily.

6 to 8 servings

Stuffed Baked Fish (Nadziewana Pieczona Ryba)

1 dressed pike, trout, or carp (4 to
    5 pounds)
    Salt and pepper
⅓ cup butter or margarine
2 onions, chopped
3 stalks celery, chopped
3 apples, cored and chopped

1. Sprinkle cavity of fish with salt and pepper.
2. For stuffing, melt ⅓ cup butter in skillet. Add onion and celery. Stir-fry until onion is transparent. Add apples, parsley, and mushrooms. Stir-fry 2 minutes longer.
3. Mix cooked vegetables with bread cubes, sugar, thyme, lemon juice, eggs, and water. Blend well.
4. Fill fish cavity with the stuffing. Close cavity with skewers

1 tablespoon chopped parsley
1 cup sliced mushrooms
4 cups dry bread cubes
2 teaspoons sugar
½ teaspoon thyme
2 teaspoons lemon juice
3 eggs
1 cup water or wine

or wooden picks. Place fish in a roasting pan and drizzle with **melted butter.**
5. Bake at 350°F about 40 minutes, or until fish flakes easily. Baste occasionally with additional melted butter.

About 8 servings

Fish in Greek Sauce (Ryba po Grecku)

1 pound carp, white fish, or
 flounder fillets
3 tablespoons olive oil
 Salt
 Fresh parsley sprigs
Greek Sauce:
 2 tablespoons olive oil
 ½ cup sliced celery
 ½ cup coarsely shredded carrots
 ½ cup coarsely shredded parsley root
 ¾ cup diced onion
 ½ cup water
 ½ teaspoon salt
 1 can (6 ounces) tomato paste
 ¼ teaspoon pepper
 ½ teaspoon sugar
 1 tablespoon lemon juice
 ½ teaspoon paprika

1. Cut fish fillets into 2-inch pieces.
2. Fry fish in hot oil in a skillet, then sprinkle with salt. Drain on paper towels. Arrange on a serving platter and keep warm. Garnish with parsley.
3. For sauce, heat oil in a skillet. Stir-fry celery, carrots, and parsley root for 3 minutes. Add onion, water, and salt. Cover; cook over low heat 15 minutes.
4. Add remaining sauce ingredients; stir to mix.
5. Chill sauce or serve hot over fish.

About 4 servings

Braised Lamb with Savoy Cabbage
(Baranina Duszona z Włoską Kapustą)

3 pounds lamb breast
1 teaspoon salt
2 cloves garlic, crushed
2 carrots
2 stalks celery with leaves
1 large onion
1 large celery root, pared
1 leek
½ parsley root
3 tablespoons butter or margarine
 Water
1 head (about 2 pounds) savoy
 cabbage, cut in quarters
1 bay leaf
½ teaspoon salt
¼ teaspoon pepper
1 tablespoon flour

1. Rub meat with 1 teaspoon salt and garlic. Let stand 1 hour.
2. Cut meat into 2-rib pieces. Dice vegetables, except for cabbage.
3. Melt 2 tablespoons butter in a large kettle. Add meat and brown. Drain off fat. Add vegetables with just enough water to cover. Simmer covered about 1 hour, or until meat is tender. Remove vegetables; discard or reserve for other use. Reduce broth to 2 cups.
4. Add cabbage and bay leaf to meat. Season with ½ teaspoon salt and pepper. Continue simmering, tightly covered, until meat and cabbage are done.
5. Blend flour into remaining 1 tablespoon butter. Stir into simmering broth. Simmer until sauce thickens, about 15 minutes.

6 servings

Braised Lamb with Caraway Seed: Prepare Braised Lamb with Savoy Cabbage, substituting **2 tablespoons caraway seed** for carrots, celery, celery root, leek, and bay leaf.

Roast Leg of Lamb (Pieczeń Baraniha z Pieca)

Vinegar
1 lamb leg, whole
Garlic cloves, slivered
Salt and pepper

1. Soak a towel with vinegar; wrap around the leg of lamb. Let stand overnight.
2. Remove towel. Trim off fell, if necessary, and excess fat. Make small slits in fat cover on meat. Push a sliver of garlic into each slit.
3. Place lamb, fat side up, on rack in a roasting pan. Sprinkle with salt and pepper.
4. Roast in a 325°F oven until done as desired. Allow 30 minutes per pound for medium; 35 minutes per pound for well-done.

About 8 to 12 servings

Flavorful pork is a gray-pink color marbled with thin streaks of pure white fat. All cuts are tender. Pork is juicier when cooked slowly for a long time than if cooked rapidly. Rapid cooking renders off fat that contains much of the flavor of pork. Pork should be cooked to the well-done stage, about 170°F on a meat thermometer.

Roast Loin of Pork (Schab Pieczony)

2 tablespoons flour
1½ teaspoons salt
1 teaspoon dry mustard or caraway seed
½ teaspoon sugar
¼ teaspoon black pepper
¼ teaspoon ground sage
1 pork loin roast (4 to 5 pounds)
Topping:
1½ cups applesauce
½ cup brown sugar
¼ teaspoon cinnamon or allspice
¼ teaspoon mace
¼ teaspoon salt

1. Mix flour, salt, mustard, sugar, pepper and sage. Rub over surface of meat. Set meat fat side up in a roasting pan.
2. Roast at 325°F 1½ hours.
3. For topping, mix applesauce with brown sugar, cinnamon, mace, and salt. Spread on top of meat.
4. Roast about 45 minutes longer, or until done.

8 to 10 servings

Sauerkraut with Pork (Kapusta z Wieprzowiną)

2 pounds pig's feet or ham hocks
2 pounds neck bones or spareribs
3 tablespoons lard or margarine
1 large onion
1 clove garlic, crushed
1½ quarts boiling water
1 green pepper, diced
4 whole allspice

1. Brown all meat in lard in a large kettle.
2. Add onion and garlic. Fry 1 minute.
3. Add boiling water, green pepper, allspice, bay leaf, and celery seed. Cover; cook 1 hour or until meat is tender.
4. Remove meat; cool. Boil until broth is reduced to 3 cups.
5. Discard bones and gristle from meat. Drain and rinse sauerkraut.
6. Cook barley in the broth 15 minutes. Add meat, sauer-

1 bay leaf
½ teaspoon celery seed
1 quart (about 2 pounds)
  sauerkraut
¼ cup barley
1 small apple, chopped
½ teaspoon caraway seed
2 teaspoons salt
½ teaspoon pepper

kraut, apple, caraway seed, salt, and pepper. Cook 45 minutes longer.
7. Serve with potato dumplings, if desired.

About 6 servings

Pork Pot Roast *(Pieczeń Wieprzowa Duszona)*

1 pork shoulder arm picnic or pork
  loin roast, boneless (3 pounds)
2 tablespoons butter or lard
2 tomatoes, peeled and cored
1 celery root
1 parsley root
1 onion, sliced
2 sprigs parsley
2 tablespoons spices to taste:
  allspice, caraway seed, whole
  cloves, juniper berries, dried
  marjoram leaves, peppercorns
  (tie in cheesecloth)
¼ cup water
½ cup bouillon or meat broth
½ cup Madeira, Marsala, or sherry

1. Rub meat with salt and pepper. Let stand 1 hour.
2. Brown meat in butter in a large, heavy skillet. Add vegetables, parsley, spice bag, and water. Cover tightly. Cook over medium heat 1½ hours; stirring as necessary and turning meat occasionally.
3. Sprinkle a small amount of flour over top of meat. Pour bouillon and wine over meat. Simmer 15 minutes.
4. Slice and arrange meat on a warm platter. Strain sauce and pour over meat.

6 to 8 servings

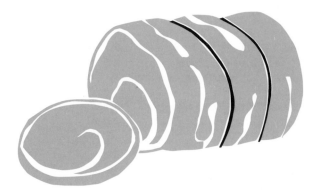

Many Polish dishes are flavored with Madeira from the Portuguese island of the same name.

Chicken Livers in Madeira Sauce
(Wątróbki z Kur w Sosie Maderowym)

1 pound chicken livers
  Milk
1 medium onion, minced
2 tablespoons chicken fat or butter
⅔ cup all-purpose flour
¾ teaspoon salt
⅔ cup chicken broth
½ cup Madeira

1. Cover chicken livers with milk; soak 2 hours. Drain; discard milk.
2. Sauté onion in fat.
3. Mix flour with salt. Coat livers with seasoned flour.
4. Add livers to onions. Stir-fry just until golden, about 5 minutes.
5. Stir in broth and wine. Cover. Simmer 5 to 10 minutes, or just until livers are tender.

4 servings

Liver à la Nelson

1½ pounds sliced calf's liver
   Milk
  6 medium potatoes, pared
  1 onion, sliced
  ½ cup sliced mushrooms
  ¼ cup butter
  ½ cup all-purpose flour
  ½ teaspoon salt
  ¼ teaspoon pepper
  1 cup bouillon or meat broth
  ½ cup sweet red wine or Madeira

1. Soak liver 45 minutes in enough milk to cover.
2. Cook potatoes in boiling water until tender; cut in thick slices.
3. Sauté onion and mushrooms in butter in a large skillet until tender, about 5 minutes.
4. Mix flour with salt and pepper. Drain liver; pat dry with paper towels. Coat liver with seasoned flour.
5. Quickly brown liver in skillet with onion and mushrooms. Add sliced potatoes, bouillon, and wine. Cover. Simmer just until liver is tender, about 10 to 15 minutes.

6 servings

Tripe and Vegetables Warsaw Style
(Flaki z Jarzynami po Warszawsku)

2 pounds fresh tripe
1 pound beef or veal soup bones
  Water
  Salt
4 carrots, sliced
1 celery root, chopped, or 3 stalks celery, sliced
1 bunch green onions, sliced
1 tablespoon chopped fresh parsley
3 cups bouillon or meat broth
2 tablespoons butter or margarine
2 tablespoons flour
½ teaspoon salt
¼ teaspoon ginger
¼ teaspoon mace
¼ teaspoon marjoram
¼ teaspoon pepper
1 cup light cream or vegetable broth

1. Clean tripe well and rinse thoroughly under running cold water.
2. Combine tripe and soup bones with enough water to cover in a large kettle. Season with ½ teaspoon salt for each cup of water added. Cover. Bring to boiling; reduce heat and simmer 3 to 5 hours, or until tripe is tender.
3. Drain tripe; discard bones and cooking liquid. Cut tripe into very thin strips.
4. Cook tripe with vegetables and parsley in bouillon until vegetables are tender.
5. Melt butter in a saucepan. Stir in flour to make a smooth paste. Cook and stir until golden. Blend in a small amount of cooking liquid. Add ½ teaspoon salt and spices. Add cream gradually, stirring until smooth.
6. Drain vegetables and tripe. Stir into sauce. Simmer 5 minutes.

4 to 6 servings

Boiled Tongue (Ozór Szpikowany w Potrawie)

1 beef tongue (about 3 pounds); fresh, smoked, or corned tongue may be used
  Boiling water
¼ pound salt pork, diced
2 onions, quartered
2 bay leaves
1 celery root or 3 stalks celery
2 carrots
2 parsnips or turnips
1 fresh horseradish root (optional)

1. Rinse tongue under cold, running water. Cook in enough boiling water to cover 1 hour.
2. Add salt pork, 1 onion, and 1 bay leaf. Cover; cook 1 to 2 hours, or until tongue is tender. Remove skin, fat, and gristle. Strain liquid.
3. Combine tongue, strained liquid, remaining onion, and bay leaf with vegetables, parsley, salt, and peppercorns. Cover; simmer until vegetables are tender, 30 to 45 minutes.
4. For sauce, purée vegetables in an electric blender or press through a sieve.
5. Combine 1½ cups cooking liquid, wine, and bouillon

1 parsley root
2 sprigs fresh parsley
1 tablespoon salt
6 whole peppercorns
Sauce:
1 cup white wine
1 bouillon cube
1 tablespoon flour
2 tablespoons butter (at room temperature)
2 tablespoons prepared cream-style horseradish

cube. Bring to boiling. Blend flour into butter; stir into boiling broth. Add vegetable purée and prepared horseradish. Cook and stir until sauce is smooth.

6. Slice tongue. Simmer in sauce 10 minutes.

About 8 servings

Polish Sausage with Red Cabbage
(Kiełbasa z Czerwoną Kapustą)

1 head red cabbage, sliced (about 2 pounds)
Boiling water
2 tablespoons butter
⅓ cup lemon juice
½ cup red wine or beef broth
½ teaspoon salt
¼ teaspoon pepper
¾ pound Polish sausage, diced
2 teaspoons brown sugar
1 tablespoon cornstarch or potato flour

1. Place cabbage in a colander. Pour boiling water over cabbage. Drain well.

2. Melt butter in a Dutch oven or large heavy skillet. Add cabbage. Stir in lemon juice. Cook and stir about 5 minutes, or until cabbage is pink. Add wine, salt, and pepper. Cover. Simmer over medium-low heat 45 minutes.

3. Mix sugar and cornstarch. Stir into simmering liquid. Bring to boiling, stirring constantly. Reduce heat; add sausage. Cover; cook 30 minutes.

About 4 servings

Sausage in Polish Sauce
(Kiełbasa w Polskim Sosie)

2 onions, sliced
3 tablespoons butter or margarine
Ring Polish sausage (about 1½ pounds)
1½ cups bouillon or meat broth
12 ounces beer
2 tablespoons flour
1 tablespoon vinegar
2 teaspoons brown sugar
¾ teaspoon salt
¼ teaspoon pepper
4 to 6 boiled potatoes

1. Sauté onion in 2 tablespoons butter until golden. Add sausage, bouillon, and beer. Simmer 20 minutes.

2. Blend flour into remaining 1 tablespoon butter. Stir into broth. Add vinegar, brown sugar, salt, and pepper.

3. Add potatoes. Cook over medium heat 10 to 15 minutes.

4. Slice sausage into 2-inch chunks to serve.

4 to 6 servings

Bacon Fry *(Grzybek ze Słoninką)*

1 pound sliced bacon, diced
4 eggs
1 cup milk
2 cups all-purpose flour
1 tablespoon sugar
2½ teaspoons baking powder
1½ teaspoons salt

1. Fry bacon just until golden in a 10-inch skillet. Remove ⅔ cup bacon and drippings.
2. Beat eggs with milk. Add 1 cup flour, sugar, baking powder, and salt. Beat until smooth. Beat in remaining flour.
3. Pour half of batter just in center of skillet over bacon and drippings. Tilt skillet slightly to spread batter. Cook until browned on bottom and set on top. Turn.
4. Sprinkle half the reserved bacon and 1 tablespoon drippings over top. Pour on half the remaining batter. Turn when bottom is browned.
5. Sprinkle remaining bacon and 2 tablespoons drippings on top. Pour on remaining batter. Turn when bottom is browned. Cook just until browned.
6. Cut into wedges for serving.

About 4 servings

Cabbage Rolls *(Gołąbki)*

1 whole head cabbage (about 3 pounds)
  Boiling water
1 pound ground beef
½ pound ground veal
¾ cup chopped onion
½ cup packaged precooked rice
1 egg, beaten
1 teaspoon salt
¼ teaspoon pepper
5 slices bacon
1 can (16 ounces) tomatoes or sauerkraut
⅓ cup bouillon or meat broth
½ teaspoon sugar
¼ teaspoon salt
¼ teaspoon pepper

1. Remove core from cabbage. Place whole head in a large kettle filled with boiling water. Cover; cook 3 minutes. Remove softened outer leaves. Repeat until all large leaves have been removed (about 20 leaves). Cut thick center stem from each slice.
2. Sauté meat with onion 5 minutes. Remove from heat. Stir in rice, egg, 1 teaspoon salt, and ¼ teaspoon pepper.
3. Place 3 tablespoons meat mixture on each cabbage leaf. Roll each leaf, tucking ends in toward center. Fasten securely with wooden picks. Place each roll seam side down in a large skillet or Dutch oven.
4. Lay bacon slices over top of cabbage rolls.
5. Mix tomatoes, bouillon, sugar, ¼ teaspoon salt, and ¼ teaspoon pepper. Pour over cabbage rolls.
6. Cover; simmer about 1 hour, turning occasionally.

About 10 servings

Cabbage Rolls with Mushroom Sauce
(Gołąbki w Grzybowym Sosie)

1 onion, chopped
1 clove garlic, crushed (optional)
2 tablespoons butter
¾ cup uncooked raw rice
½ pound ground beef or veal
½ pound ground pork
1 teaspoon salt
¼ teaspoon pepper
1 whole head cabbage (about 3 pounds)

1. Sauté onion and garlic in butter in a large skillet, about 5 minutes. Add rice, meat, salt, and pepper. Stir-fry just to mix well. Remove from heat.
2. Remove core from cabbage. Place whole head in a large kettle filled with boiling water. Cover; cook 3 minutes. Remove softened outer leaves. Repeat until all leaves are softened and have been removed. Cut thick stem from each leaf.
3. Taking one large cabbage leaf at a time, spoon about 1 rounded tablespoonful of meat mixture in center of leaf.

Boiling water
2 cups beef broth or stock
1 can (about 10 ounces) condensed
    cream of mushroom soup

Cover with a small leaf. Tuck ends up and just over edge of filling; place one end of leaf over filling and roll up loosely. If desired, secure with a wooden pick. Repeat until all filling and leaves are used. Place cabbage rolls in a large casserole; do not make more than 2 layers.

4. Combine beef broth and mushroom soup; pour over cabbage rolls.

5. Bake at 350°F about 1½ hours.

8 to 12 servings

Stuffed Cabbage Rolls *(Gołąbki)*

1 whole head cabbage (about 4
    pounds)
    Boiling salted water
1 onion, chopped
2 tablespoons oil
1½ pounds ground beef
½ pound ground fresh pork
1½ cups cooked rice
1 teaspoon salt
¼ teaspoon pepper
2 cans (about 10 ounces each)
    condensed tomato soup
2½ cups water

1. Remove core from cabbage. Place whole head in a large kettle filled with boiling salted water. Cover; cook 3 minutes, or until softened enough to pull off individual leaves. Repeat to remove all large leaves (about 30). Cut thick center stem from each leaf. Chop remaining cabbage.

2. Sauté onion in oil. Add meat, rice, salt, and pepper. Mix thoroughly. Place a heaping tablespoonful of meat mixture on each cabbage leaf. Tuck sides over filling while rolling leaf around filling. Secure with wooden picks.

3. Place half the chopped cabbage on bottom of a large Dutch oven. Fill with layers of the cabbage rolls. Cover with remaining chopped cabbage.

4. Combine tomato soup with water; mix until smooth. Pour over cabbage rolls. Cover and bring to boiling. Reduce heat and simmer 1½ hours.

5. Serve cabbage rolls with the sauce.

About 15 servings

Royal Chicken

⅓ cup butter
2 medium onions, chopped
1 cup sliced mushrooms
1 chicken or capon, cut in pieces
1 cup hot water
1 teaspoon salt
¼ teaspoon pepper
1 tablespoon flour
1 teaspoon paprika (optional)
1 cup dairy sour cream or white
    wine

1. Melt butter in a large skillet. Add onion, mushrooms, and chicken pieces. Stir-fry until golden.

2. Add water, salt, and pepper.

3. Cover; cook over medium heat about 35 minutes, or until chicken is tender.

4. Blend flour, paprika (if desired), and sour cream. Stir into liquid in skillet. Bring just to boiling. Simmer 3 minutes.

About 6 servings

Smothered Stuffed Chicken
(Nadziewane Kurczątko Duszone)

1 chicken (about 3 pounds)
½ teaspoon salt
⅛ teaspoon pepper
2 tablespoons butter
1¼ cups dry bread cubes or pieces
¼ cup chopped onion
½ teaspoon dill weed
¼ cup hot milk
⅓ cup butter, melted

1. Sprinkle inside of chicken with salt and pepper. Tuck wing tips underneath wings. Chop liver.
2. Sauté liver in 2 tablespoons butter 2 minutes. Add bread cubes, onion, dill, and milk; mix.
3. Stuff chicken. Close and secure with poultry pins. Place in a ceramic or earthenware casserole.
4. Pour melted butter over chicken. Cover.
5. Bake at 350°F about 1 hour, or until chicken is tender.
6. If desired, remove cover. Baste. Increase temperature to 450°F. Bake 10 minutes to brown.

4 to 6 servings

Chicken with Anchovies
(Pularda Pieczona z Sardelami)

1 chicken (3 pounds), split in half
1 can (2 ounces) flat anchovy
    fillets, cut in half
1 cup chicken broth
1 tablespoon lemon juice
1 slice bacon, chopped
    Hot cooked rice
¼ cup dairy sour cream
¼ teaspoon ginger

1. Slit the skin of the chickens, and insert anchovies in slits as in larding meat.
2. Put chicken, broth, lemon juice, and bacon into a flame-proof casserole or Dutch oven. Cover; simmer about 1 hour, or until chicken is tender.
3. Spoon hot rice onto platter. Set chicken on rice.
4. Blend sour cream and ginger into liquid in casserole. Heat just until mixture bubbles; do not boil. Serve sauce over chicken.

4 to 6 servings

Chicken Polish Style (Kurczęta po Polsku)

1 chicken (2 to 3 pounds)
    Salt
    Chicken livers
¾ cup dry bread crumbs
1 egg
1 teaspoon dill weed
¼ teaspoon pepper
½ cup milk (about)
⅓ cup melted butter

1. Sprinkle the chicken with salt. Let stand 1 hour.
2. Chop the livers finely. Combine with bread crumbs, egg, salt to taste, dill, pepper, and as much milk as needed for a loose, sour-cream-like consistency.
3. Fill cavity of chicken with crumb mixture; truss. Place chicken in roasting pan.
4. Bake at 400°F about 45 minutes, or until chicken is tender. Baste often with melted butter.

About 4 servings

Chicken with Ham: Prepare Chicken Polish Style as directed. Substitute **6 ounces (1 cup) ground ham, ½ cup sliced mushrooms,** and **2 crushed juniper berries** for the chicken livers. Add **½ cup sherry** to pan drippings for a sauce.

Roast Turkey with Anchovies
(Pieczony Indyk z Sardelami)

1 turkey (12 to 15 pounds)
5 slices bacon
1 large onion, minced
¾ pound veal (2 cups ground)
3 slices stale bread, cubed
⅓ cup milk or chicken broth
1 can (2 ounces) flat anchovies
2 tablespoons butter
2 eggs, beaten
  Grated peel and juice of 1 lemon
½ teaspoon pepper
⅔ cup melted butter

1. Rinse turkey with running water. Dry with paper towels.
2. Dice bacon. Fry until transparent. Add onion; stir-fry until golden. Stir in veal, bread cubes, and milk. Remove from heat.
3. Finely chop or mash anchovies. Mix in butter, lemon peel and juice, and pepper; beat until well combined. Add to meat mixture and stir until well blended. Stuffing should be of a paste consistency.
4. Spread stuffing in cavity of turkey. Truss.
5. Place turkey in roasting pan. If desired, insert meat thermometer in thickest part of breast.
6. Roast at 425°F about 3½ hours, basting frequently with melted butter and pan drippings. When done, leg of turkey moves easily and meat thermometer registers 180° to 185°F.

12 to 18 servings

Smothered Duck in Caper Sauce
(Kaczka Duszona w Sosie Kaparowym)

1 duck (5 to 6 pounds), cut up
1 clove garlic, crushed (optional)
  Salt and pepper
3 tablespoons butter or bacon
  drippings
1 cup chicken or beef bouillon
2 tablespoons water
2 teaspoons cornstarch
⅓ cup capers
2 teaspoons brown or caramelized
  sugar
1 tablespoon lemon juice

1. Rub duck with garlic. Sprinkle cavity with salt and pepper to taste. Let stand 1 to 2 hours.
2. Melt butter in a heavy skillet or Dutch oven. Add duck and brown quickly on all sides. Drain off fat, if desired.
3. Add bouillon. Cover. Simmer over medium heat about 1 hour, or until duck is tender.
4. Remove duck to a heated platter.
5. Blend water into cornstarch. Stir into hot liquid in Dutch oven. Add capers, cook and stir over high heat until sauce boils. Reduce heat. Add sugar and lemon juice. Stir just until sauce is thickened.

About 4 servings

Duck with Red Cabbage
(Kaczka Duszona z Kapustą)

1 head red cabbage, shredded
1 onion, chopped
  Salt
6 ounces salt pork, diced
½ cup red wine or chicken broth
1 duck (5 to 6 pounds)

1. Put cabbage and onion into a bowl, sprinkle with salt, and let stand 10 minutes. Squeeze out liquid.
2. Fry salt pork in a skillet until golden. Add cabbage-onion mixture and wine. Cover and simmer 20 minutes.
3. Place duck in a roasting pan.
4. Bake at 425°F 30 minutes. Drain off fat. Spoon cabbage mixture over duck. Reduce oven temperature to 350°F. Bake about 45 minutes, or until duck is tender. Baste frequently.

About 4 servings

Capon in Cream *(Kapłon z Kremem z Pieca)*

1 capon or chicken (5 to 6 pounds)
  Salt
2 cups chicken stock or broth
4 egg yolks
1 tablespoon melted butter
4 teaspoons flour
2 cups dairy sour cream
1 teaspoon salt
¼ teaspoon pepper

1. Sprinkle cavity of bird with salt. Place in a large kettle.
2. Add stock to kettle. Cover. Simmer until just tender (about 1 hour). Allow to cool.
3. Meanwhile, cream egg yolks and butter; add flour and blend thoroughly. Stir in sour cream. Season with 1 teaspoon salt and pepper. Beat at high speed until stiff. Cook until thickened in top of a double boiler, stirring constantly to keep from curdling or sticking (handle like hollandaise sauce). Cool.
4. Make cuts in capon as for carving, but without cutting through. Place in a shallow baking pan. Fill cuts with sauce, then spread remainder over the whole surface of the bird.
5. Bake at 425°F about 20 minutes, or until sauce is browned.
6. Meanwhile, boil liquid in which chicken was cooked until it is reduced to 1 cup of stock.
7. To serve, pour stock over capon. Carve at the table.

About 6 servings

Potted Pheasant *(Bażant Pieczony)*

¾ cup all-purpose flour
½ teaspoon salt
¼ teaspoon pepper
1 pheasant, cut in pieces
½ cup butter
1 onion, quartered
1 stalk celery, cut up
2 cups meat stock or beef broth
3 whole allspice
½ cup whipping cream
2 tablespoons sherry

1. Mix flour with salt and pepper.
2. Coat each piece of pheasant with seasoned flour. Melt butter in a Dutch oven or flameproof casserole. Brown pheasant in butter. Add onion, celery, and 1 cup meat stock. Cover.
3. Bake at 350°F 40 minutes. Add remaining meat stock. Do not cover. Bake about 40 minutes longer, or until pheasant is tender.
4. Remove pheasant to heated platter. Strain broth; combine 1 cup broth with cream and sherry. Serve over the pheasant.

2 to 4 servings

Smothered Pigeons *(Potrawka z Gołębi)*

3 tablespoons butter
2 pigeons (about 2 pounds)
3 onions, sliced
1 cup meat stock or broth
2 tart apples, cored and sliced
¼ cup sliced mushrooms
  Juice of ½ lemon
⅓ cup Madeira
1 tablespoon butter or margarine
   (at room temperature)
1 tablespoon Browned Flour
1 cup dairy sour cream

1. Melt butter in a large skillet. Sauté pigeons in butter 15 minutes. Remove pigeons.
2. Fry onions in the butter left in skillet until tender. Add stock, sliced apples, mushrooms, and lemon juice. Mix well and bring to boiling. Add wine.
3. Mix butter with flour until smooth. Stir into liquid in skillet. Cook and stir until mixture is thickened.
4. Dip pigeons in sour cream; return to skillet. Cook, covered, until tender.

2 servings

Browned Flour: Spread **1½ cups all-purpose flour** in a shallow baking pan. Place on lowest position for broiler. Broil and stir about 20 minutes, or until flour is golden brown. Stirring must be almost constant to prevent burning. If flour burns, skim off burned portion and continue browning remainder. Cool. Store in tightly covered container.

About 1⅓ cups

Baked Pigeon *(Gołąb Pieczony)*

1 pigeon
Salt and pepper
1 strip bacon, diced
Melted butter

1. Soak the pigeon about 2 hours in cold water. Dry with paper towels.
2. Sprinkle cavity with salt and pepper.
3. Make small slits in skin; insert pieces of bacon. Place in a roasting pan.
4. Bake at 350°F 30 to 40 minutes, or until tender; baste often with butter.

1 serving

Wild Duck, Goose, or Partridge
(Dzika Kaczka, Gęś, lub Kuropatwy)

2 partridges, 1 duck, or 1 goose
12 peppercorns
1 onion, quartered
Salt
14 to 20 juniper seeds, ground or mashed
2 tablespoons bacon drippings or butter
½ cup water
2 cups sliced red cabbage
1 large onion, sliced
½ cup water
1 tablespoon cornstarch or potato starch
2 tablespoons water
½ teaspoon sugar
1 teaspoon vinegar
¾ cup red wine

1. Place partridges in a plastic bag with peppercorns and quartered onion. Refrigerate 3 days to age.
2. Discard peppercorns and quartered onion. Cut up bird. Sprinkle with salt and juniper. Let stand 1 hour.
3. Heat bacon drippings in a large skillet. Brown bird in the drippings; add ½ cup water. Cover and simmer 1 hour.
4. Add cabbage, sliced onion, and ½ cup water. Cover and simmer 30 minutes. Remove the meat to a warmed platter.
5. Mix the cornstarch with 2 tablespoons water to make a smooth paste. Stir into drippings in pan.
6. Stir in sugar and vinegar; bring to boiling. Cook and stir 2 minutes. Remove from heat. Stir in wine.

4 servings

Rabbit *(Zając Pieczony)*

1 rabbit (2 to 3 pounds), cut in pieces
Salt and pepper
Flour
¼ cup butter
1 cup chopped mushrooms
1 onion, sliced
1 clove garlic, sliced
1 cup meat stock
⅔ cup dry white wine*
½ teaspoon ground thyme
2 bay leaves
Sauce:
1 cup dairy sour cream
1 teaspoon dried parsley flakes
¼ teaspoon nutmeg

* Or substitute ½ cup water and 1 tablespoon lemon juice

1. Sprinkle rabbit pieces with salt and pepper. Coat with flour.
2. Melt butter in a Dutch oven or flame-proof casserole. Add mushrooms, onion, and garlic. Add rabbit pieces and brown quickly. Remove garlic.
3. Mix stock with wine, thyme, and bay leaves. Add to rabbit.
4. Bake at 350°F or simmer about 1½ hours, or until rabbit is very tender.
5. Remove rabbit and place on heated platter. Stir sauce ingredients into broth in pan. Cook and stir just until sauce begins to simmer. Spoon over rabbit.

4 to 6 servings

Leg of Venison *(Sarna Duszona)*

Marinade:
- 1 bottle (4/5 quart) dry white wine
- 3 cups vinegar
- 2 cups olive oil or salad oil
- 1 cup sliced carrots
- 1 cup sliced onions
- 2 stalks celery, cut in pieces
- 2 cloves garlic, crushed
- 3 sprigs parsley
- 1 bay leaf
- 6 whole cloves
- 6 peppercorns

Venison and Sauce:
- 1 leg of venison (5 to 6 pounds)
- ¼ cup oil
- 2 tablespoons butter
- 1 onion, diced
- 1 cup red wine
- 3 tablespoons sugar
- 6 whole cloves
- 1 cup dairy sour cream
- ½ cup all-purpose flour
- Salt and pepper

1. Combine all ingredients for marinade in a large crock. Soak the venison 2 or 3 days in the marinade. Remove and wipe dry with a cloth.
2. Heat oil and butter in a heavy skillet. Add venison; brown evenly on all sides. Fry onion in the same butter.
3. Strain 1 cup marinade. Add to skillet.
4. Place venison in a Dutch oven or roaster. Add liquid and onion from skillet. Add wine, sugar, and cloves.
5. Cover; simmer or bake at 350°F about 2½ hours, or until meat is tender.
6. Remove venison to carving board.
7. Make sauce by combining sour cream and flour. Gradually stir in 1 cup strained cooking broth. Return to Dutch oven; cook, stirring, until smooth and thick. Season to taste with salt and pepper.
8. To serve, carve venison; place slices on a warmed platter. Pour sauce over top.

8 to 12 servings

Veal à la Nelson *(Zrazy po Nelsońsku)*

- 3 ounces dried mushrooms (optional)
- 2 cups warm milk
- 3 slices bacon
- 1 pound fresh mushrooms, sliced
- 4 large onions, chopped
- 8 veal cutlets (about 3 pounds)
- 3 bouillon cubes
- 3 tablespoons flour
- ¼ cup butter or margarine, melted
- 1 cup dairy sour cream
- Salt and pepper
- 8 medium potatoes, cooked

1. Soak dried mushrooms in warm milk 2 hours.
2. Fry bacon in a large skillet. Add mushrooms and onion. Sauté until onion is soft. Add fried bacon, mushrooms, and onion to milk.
3. Sauté veal in drippings. Add oil, if needed.
4. Add milk mixture and bouillon cubes. Cover; simmer 1 hour.
5. Stir flour into melted butter. Blend in a small amount of cooking liquid. Stir into remainder of liquid in skillet. Cook and stir until sauce is smooth and thick. Then blend in sour cream. Season to taste with salt and pepper.
6. Add potatoes. Cook 10 to 15 minutes, or until potatoes are hot.

8 servings

Polish Noodles and Cabbage
(Kluski z Kapustą po Polski)

- ¼ cup butter or margarine
- ½ cup chopped onion
- 4 cups chopped or sliced cabbage
- 1 teaspoon caraway seed
- ½ teaspoon salt
- ⅛ teaspoon pepper
- 1 package (8 ounces) egg noodles
- ½ cup dairy sour cream (optional)

1. Melt butter in a large skillet. Add onion; sauté until soft.
2. Add cabbage; sauté 5 minutes, or until crisp-tender. Stir in caraway seed, salt, and pepper.
3. Meanwhile, cook noodles in salted boiling water as directed on package. Drain well.
4. Stir noodles into cabbage. Add sour cream, if desired. Cook 5 minutes longer, stirring frequently.

6 to 8 servings

VEGETABLES, SALADS, SAUCES, AND DRESSINGS

An Italian queen is credited with adding vegetables to Polish cuisine, but the Poles have long since given them a magic refinement. Cucumbers in Sour Cream are refreshing, Mushroom Cutlets buttery rich, and the sauerkraut dishes unlike any other you have tasted. The Rose Salad makes a stunning buffet decoration. Cold horseradish sauce is a natural with cold meat, as is the tartar sauce with fish.

Mushroom Cutlets *(Kotlety z Grzybów)*

1 pound fresh mushrooms or 2 cups drained canned mushrooms
1 cup chopped onion
2 tablespoons butter
2 cups stale bread cubes
½ cup milk or water
3 eggs, beaten
1 tablespoon chopped parsley
½ teaspoon salt
¼ teaspoon pepper
Fine dry bread crumbs

1. Chop mushrooms. Sauté with onion in butter.
2. Soak bread cubes in milk 10 minutes. Add to mushrooms. Stir in eggs, parsley, salt, and pepper.
3. Shape into patties, using about 3 tablespoons for each. Coat with bread crumbs.
4. Fry in **butter** in a skillet until golden brown on both sides.

About 12 to 14 cutlets

Baked Mushroom Mounds: Prepare Mushroom Cutlets as directed; add ¼ **teaspoon mace** along with salt. Spoon mushroom mixture into well-greased muffin pans. Dot tops with small pieces of **butter.** Bake at 350°F 15 to 20 minutes, or until set.

Beets *(Buraki)*

6 cooked beets, peeled
2 tablespoons butter
1 tablespoon flour
1 tablespoon vinegar
½ teaspoon salt
1 tablespoon sugar
¼ teaspoon caraway seed
½ cup dairy sour cream

1. Grate the beets.
2. Melt butter in a saucepan; add flour and blend. Stir in vinegar, salt, sugar, and caraway seed.
3. Add beets. Cook over high heat 2 or 3 minutes. Stir in sour cream. Serve at once.

4 servings

Cucumbers in Sour Cream (Mizeria ze Śmietaną)

3 cups sliced cucumbers
Salt
¼ cup chopped fresh dill or 2 tablespoons dill weed
1 cup dairy sour cream or yogurt

1. Sprinkle cucumbers with salt. Let stand 30 minutes. Pat dry with paper towels.
2. Stir dill into sour cream. Add cucumbers; mix well.

4 to 6 servings

Radishes with Sour Cream: Follow directions for Cucumbers in Sour Cream; substitute **radishes** for cucumbers and omit step 1.

Vegetables Polonaise (Jarzyny po Polsku)

1½ pounds vegetables (Brussels sprouts or savoy cabbage or carrots or cauliflower or green beans or leeks)
1 cup boiling water
1 teaspoon salt
½ teaspoon sugar (optional)
2 tablespoons butter
¼ teaspoon salt
⅛ teaspoon pepper
1 tablespoon lemon juice (optional)
2 tablespoons fine dry bread crumbs

1. Choose one vegetable to prepare at a time. Trim and pare as necessary. (Leave Brussels sprouts and green beans whole. Cut cabbage into six wedges. Leave cauliflower whole or break into flowerets. Slice leeks.)
2. Cook vegetable, covered, in boiling water with 1 teaspoon salt and the sugar, if desired, until tender. Drain off water.
3. Melt butter. Stir in ¼ teaspoon salt, pepper, and lemon juice. Add bread crumbs. Sauté until golden. Spoon over top of vegetable.

About 4 servings

Sauerkraut (Kapusta Kiszona)

1 pound sauerkraut, drained
5 slices bacon, diced
1½ cups water
1 tablespoon flour
½ cup dairy sour cream (optional)

1. Rinse sauerkraut if mild favor is desired. Drain well.
2. Fry bacon in a skillet until golden. Drain off 1 tablespoon fat; set aside.
3. Add sauerkraut to skillet. Fry 3 minutes, stirring often.
4. Add water. Cover and cook 45 minutes over medium heat.
5. Blend flour into reserved bacon fat. Stir into sauerkraut. Cook and stir over high heat 2 minutes. Stir in sour cream, if desired. Remove from heat.

About 4 servings

Stuffed Tomatoes (Pomidory Faszerowane)

4 medium tomatoes
⅓ cup chopped onion
2 tablespoons butter or margarine
½ pound ground beef or pork (optional)
1 cup cooked rice
1 tablespoon chopped fresh dill or 1 teaspoon dill weed
½ teaspoon salt
¼ teaspoon pepper
⅓ cup dairy sour cream
Fine dry bread crumbs

1. Remove cores and seeds from tomatoes.
2. Sauté onion in butter. Add meat; cook until browned. Add rice, dill, salt, pepper, and sour cream; mix well.
3. Stuff tomatoes with rice mixture. Sprinkle bread crumbs on top. Place in a shallow casserole or baking dish. Cover.
4. Bake at 375°F 20 minutes. Remove cover. Continue baking until tender.

4 servings

Note: Green peppers may be substituted for tomatoes, if desired.

Smothered Green Peas or Salad Greens
(Groszek Zielony lub Sałata Duszona)

2 packages (10 ounces each) frozen
    peas or 1¼ pounds escarole or
    endive, trimmed
1 teaspoon salt
2 cups boiling water
½ cup dairy sour cream
1 teaspoon dill weed
2 tablespoons melted butter or
    bacon drippings
2 tablespoons flour
¼ teaspoon pepper
1 tablespoon chopped parsley

1. Add peas and salt to boiling water. Cover; remove from heat. Let stand 10 minutes. Drain.
2. Combine sour cream, dill weed, butter, flour, pepper, and parsley; mix well. Add to vegetables. Cover. Cook over medium-low heat 10 to 15 minutes, or until tender; stirring occasionally. Garnish with croutons, if desired.

4 to 6 servings

Stuffed Vegetables (Jarzyny Faszerowane)

6 turnips, kohlrabi, cucumbers, or
    celery roots (about 1½
    pounds)
2 cups boiling water or chicken
    broth
1½ teaspoons salt
½ teaspoon sugar (optional)
¼ pound ground beef or pork
¼ cup sliced mushrooms
¼ cup chopped onion
1 tablespoon grated Parmesan
    cheese (optional)
¼ teaspoon salt
⅛ teaspoon pepper
1 egg, beaten
2 tablespoons fine dry bread
    crumbs

1. Trim and pare vegetables. Cook in boiling water with 1½ teaspoons salt and sugar, if desired, until tender.
2. Scoop out centers of vegetables until a thick, hollow shell is left.
3. Fry ground beef with mushrooms and onion in a skillet until onion is golden. Add cheese, salt, and pepper; mix well. Remove from heat. Blend in egg.
4. Mash scooped-out portion of vegetables. Combine with meat mixture.
5. Fill vegetable shells with stuffing. Sprinkle bread crumbs on top.
6. Place stuffed vegetables in a shallow casserole or baking dish.
7. Bake at 400°F 10 to 15 minutes, or until lightly browned on top.

6 servings

Smothered Vegetables (Jarzyny Duszone)

1½ pounds potatoes, carrots,
    turnips, or celery roots
1 cup boiling water
1 teaspoon salt
4 teaspoons butter
4 teaspoons flour
¼ teaspoon pepper
1 tablespoon lemon juice
    (optional)
1 cup bouillon

1. Choose one vegetable to prepare at a time. Pare and slice or dice. Cook in boiling water with 1 teaspoon salt about 10 minutes, until crisp-tender. Drain.
2. Melt butter in a saucepan. Stir in flour, pepper, and, if desired, lemon juice. Gradually stir in bouillon. Add vegetable; stir to coat with sauce.
3. Cook, covered, 15 minutes, or until vegetable is tender. Garnish with Croutons (page 30), if desired.

About 4 servings

Note: For extra flavor, dice **2 slices bacon.** Stir-fry until golden but not crisp. Substitute for butter.

Stuffed Artichokes or Tomatoes
(Karczochy lub Pomidory Faszerowane)

4 cooked artichokes or 4 small
    tomatoes
¾ cup chopped onion
1 clove garlic, crushed
2 tablespoons butter
⅓ cup fine dry bread crumbs
1 tablespoon chopped fresh parsley
½ teaspoon dried basil leaves
½ teaspoon salt
¼ teaspoon pepper
1 tablespoon grated Parmesan
    cheese (optional)
4 teaspoons butter or margarine

1. Remove center leaves of artichokes; remove chokes. (Remove core from tomatoes and scoop out seeds; sprinkle inside with sugar and salt.)
2. Sauté onion and garlic in 2 tablespoons butter. Stir in bread crumbs, parsley, basil, salt, and pepper.
3. Fill vegetables with onion mixture. Sprinkle cheese on top. Set in a shallow casserole or baking dish. Place 1 teaspoon butter on top of each stuffed vegetable.
4. Bake at 375°F about 20 minutes, or until tender and browned on top.

4 servings

Warsaw Salad (Sałatka Warszawska)

1 cup mayonnaise
⅓ cup dairy sour cream
1 tablespoon prepared mustard
2 cups julienne beets, cooked or
    canned
1½ cups kidney beans, cooked or
    canned
1½ cups cooked or canned peas
1 cup diced dill pickles
6 ounces (about 1¼ cups) cooked
    crab meat
3 scallions, chopped
1 hard-cooked egg, sliced
    Carrot curls and radish roses to
    garnish

1. Combine mayonnaise, sour cream, and mustard in a large bowl.
2. Add remaining ingredients, except egg, carrots, and radishes; toss gently to mix.
3. Garnish with egg slices, carrot curls, and radish roses.

8 to 12 servings

Sauerkraut Salad with Carrots and Apples
(Surówka z Kiszonej Kapusty)

¼ cup salad or olive oil
1½ teaspoons sugar
1 teaspoon caraway seed
½ teaspoon salt
1 teaspoon vinegar
1 pound sauerkraut, drained
2 medium tart apples, peeled,
    cored, and diced
¾ cup grated carrot

1. Combine oil, sugar, caraway seed, salt, and vinegar.
2. Rinse and drain sauerkraut well; chop. Stir into oil mixture.
3. Add apples and carrot; toss to mix.

About 6 servings

Potato Salad with Wine
(Sałatka Kartoflana z Winem)

2 pounds potatoes
2 teaspoons salt
  Boiling water
1 cup white wine
1 stalk celery
⅓ cup olive oil
¼ cup chopped fresh dill
¼ cup chopped parsley
3 tablespoons lemon juice
2 tablespoons chopped chives
¼ teaspoon pepper

1. Cook potatoes with salt in enough boiling water to cover until tender, about 30 minutes. Peel and slice; put into a bowl.
2. Pour wine over potatoes; let stand 30 minutes.
3. Cook celery in a small amount of boiling water until soft. Press celery through a sieve. Combine 2 tablespoons cooking liquid with puréed celery, oil, dill, parsley, lemon juice, chives, and pepper.
4. Add celery mixture to potatoes; mix.

6 servings

Rose Salad

10 small potatoes (about 2½ pounds), cooked
¼ cup olive oil
3 tablespoons lemon juice or vinegar
1 tablespoon water
1 tablespoon sugar
1 teaspoon salt
¼ teaspoon pepper
2 cups shell beans, cooked or canned
¼ pound sauerkraut, drained
4 stalks celery, sliced lengthwise
6 cups shredded red cabbage
  Boiling water
3 tablespoons tarragon vinegar
4 cooked or canned beets, sliced

1. Slice potatoes. Mix olive oil, lemon juice, 1 tablespoon water, sugar, salt, and pepper. Pour over potatoes. Add beans, sauerkraut, and celery.
2. Add red cabbage to boiling water. Let stand 2 minutes. Drain well. Stir in tarragon vinegar; mix until cabbage is pink.
3. Mound red cabbage in center of a large platter. Arrange beet slices in cabbage to form a rose.
4. Place potatoes and other vegetables around edges. Use **celery** for rose stem. Garnish with **lettuce leaves.**

8 to 12 servings

Mustard Sauce (Sos Musztardowy)

¾ cup dairy sour cream
⅓ cup mayonnaise
2 tablespoons prepared mustard
¼ teaspoon salt
¼ teaspoon sugar

1. Mix all ingredients well.
2. Serve with cold pork, ham, or hard-cooked eggs.

About 1¼ cups

Sour Cream Sauce (Sos Śmietanowy)

2 hard-cooked eggs
1 cup dairy sour cream
1 teaspoon prepared mustard or dill
¼ teaspoon sugar
¼ teaspoon salt
⅛ teaspoon pepper

1. Press eggs through a sieve. Add sour cream and beat with a mixer at medium speed 3 minutes. Add mustard, sugar, salt, and pepper. Beat 1 minute at high speed.
2. Serve with ham or veal.

1½ cups

Mushroom Sauce (Sos Grzybowy)

1 pound mushrooms, sliced
1 large onion, chopped
1 cup chicken or meat broth or bouillon
3 tablespoons flour
2 tablespoons melted butter
½ cup dairy sour cream
1 teaspoon lemon juice
Salt and pepper

1. Simmer mushrooms with onion in bouillon 15 minutes.
2. Blend flour into butter. Stir into mushrooms. Bring to boiling, stirring.
3. Remove from heat. Stir in sour cream, lemon juice, and salt and pepper to taste.

3 cups

Green Onion Sauce (Sos Szczypiorkowy)

1 cup dairy sour cream
3 tablespoons sliced green onion
1 egg yolk, beaten
2 tablespoons prepared mustard
1 teaspoon lemon juice
½ teaspoon sugar
¼ teaspoon salt

1. Combine sour cream, green onion, egg yolk, prepared mustard, lemon juice, sugar, and salt.
2. Serve hot or cold.

About 1⅓ cups

Cold Horseradish Sauce (Sos Chrzanowy Zimny)

6 ounces prepared cream-style horseradish
1 large apple, pared and shredded
1½ cups dairy sour cream
½ teaspoon sugar
¼ teaspoon salt

1. Mix horseradish with apple. Add sour cream; stir in sugar and salt.
2. Serve with cold meat, hard-cooked eggs, and fish.

About 2½ cups

Tartar Sauce (Sos Tatarski)

2 hard-cooked eggs
2 tablespoons finely chopped mushrooms
2 tablespoons salad oil
2 teaspoons prepared mustard
2 teaspoons pickle liquid
¼ teaspoon salt
¼ teaspoon sugar
½ cup mayonnaise
½ cup dairy sour cream
¼ cup finely chopped dill pickles

1. Mash cooked egg yolks. Chop whites separately.
2. Sauté mushrooms in oil. Blend in mashed egg yolks, mustard, pickle liquid, salt, and sugar.
3. Blend mayonnaise into sour cream. Add chopped egg whites, egg yolk mixture, and pickles; mix well.

About 2 cups

A Polish tablecloth over 100 years old, a metal-encrusted wooden tray, and a doll in typical folk costume surround **Cauliflower Polonaise, 60.**

DESSERTS

Poles take special pride in their desserts. Their pastries, in particular, can rival those of any other cuisine in the world. Mazurkas are a special treat. Try the several variations of this cookielike pastry. You will certainly be congratulated for your chocolate or walnut tortes and possibly even more so for the Country Cheese Cake. For special occasions the Baba (grandmother) cake is a must.

Polish Pecan Cookies (Ciastka Kurche)

1 cup butter
3 tablespoons vanilla extract
½ cup confectioners' sugar
1½ tablespoons water
2½ cups sifted all-purpose flour
2 cups pecan halves
Confectioners' sugar for rolling

1. Cream butter with vanilla extract; add confectioners' sugar gradually, beating until fluffy.
2. Add water and beat thoroughly.
3. Add flour in fourths, mixing until blended after each addition.
4. If necessary, chill the dough until easy to handle.
5. Shape a teaspoonful of dough around each pecan half, covering nut completely. Place on ungreased cookie sheets.
6. Bake at 400°F 10 minutes.
7. Roll in confectioners' sugar while still warm.

About 5 dozen

Butter Horns (Rogaliki)

1 cup sweet unsalted butter or margarine
½ cup sugar
1 egg yolk
1 teaspoon vanilla extract
¼ cup chopped blanched almonds
1⅔ cups all-purpose flour
Confectioners' sugar

1. Beat butter at high speed and add sugar gradually, creaming until light and fluffy. Beat in egg yolk and vanilla extract. Beat in almonds, then flour.
2. With hands, shape 1-inch pieces of dough into crescents. Place on ungreased baking sheets, about 1 inch apart.
3. Bake at 350°F about 20 minutes, or until just golden on edges.
4. While warm, coat crescents with confectioners' sugar.

About 3 dozen

A peacock's feather is a good-luck charm. Lucky guests will feast on **Chocolate Torte, 70,** or **Walnut Torte, 71**

Polish Doughnuts (Pączki)

1 package active dry yeast
¼ cup warm water
⅓ cup butter or margarine (at room temperature)
⅔ cup sugar
1 egg
3 egg yolks
1 teaspoon vanilla extract
1 teaspoon grated orange or lemon peel
¾ teaspoon salt
3½ cups all-purpose flour (about)
   Fat for deep frying heated to 375°F
   Confectioners' sugar (optional)

1. Dissolve yeast in warm water.
2. Cream butter and sugar until fluffy. Beat in egg, then egg yolks, one at a time. Add vanilla extract, orange peel, dissolved yeast, and salt. Beat until well mixed. Stir in flour gradually, adding enough to make a stiff dough.
3. Turn dough onto a floured surface. Knead until smooth and elastic, about 10 minutes. Place in a greased bowl. Cover. Let rise until doubled in bulk.
4. Turn onto lightly floured surface. Pat or roll to ½-inch thickness. Cut out with doughnut cutter. Cover. Let rise until doubled in bulk.
5. Fry in hot fat 2 to 3 minutes; turn to brown all sides.
6. Drain doughnuts on paper towels and sprinkle with confectioners' sugar, if desired.

About 2 dozen

Wise Men (Mądrzyki)

1 pound farmer or pot cheese
4 eggs, separated
3 tablespoons sugar
¼ teaspoon salt
¼ cup all-purpose flour
   Fat for deep frying heated to 365°F
   Dairy sour cream and sugar (optional)

1. Press cheese through a sieve.
2. Combine egg yolks and sugar; beat at high speed until mixture is thick and piles softly, about 7 minutes.
3. Add cheese and salt, then mix in flour, 1 tablespoon at a time. Add just enough flour to form a dough. (Dough will be sticky.)
4. Pat out dough on generously floured surface to ¾-inch thickness.
5. Cut into 2×1-inch rectangles with well-floured knife.
6. Fry the rectangles quickly, turning to brown both sides. (Be sure the temperature of the fat is maintained at 365°F, so the cheese will fry crisply.)
7. Serve at once with dairy sour cream and sugar, if desired.

About 2½ dozen

Favors (Chrust-Faworki)

4 egg yolks
1 whole egg
½ teaspoon salt
⅓ cup confectioners' sugar
2 tablespoons rum or brandy
1 teaspoon vanilla extract
1¼ cups all-purpose flour
   Fat for deep frying heated to 350°F
   Confectioners' sugar or honey for topping (optional)

1. Combine egg yolks, whole egg, and salt in small bowl of electric mixer. Beat at highest speed 7 to 10 minutes, until mixture is thick and piles softly. Beat in sugar, a small amount at a time. Then beat in rum and vanilla extract.
2. By hand, fold in flour.
3. Turn onto a generously floured surface. Knead dough until blisters form, about 10 minutes.
4. Divide dough in half. Cover half of dough to prevent drying. Use a towel or plastic wrap.
5. Roll out half of dough as thin as possible. Cut dough into 5×2-inch strips. Make a 2-inch slit from center almost to end of each strip of dough. Then pull opposite end through slit. Repeat with remaining dough.
6. Fry in hot fat until golden brown.
7. Drain on paper towels. If desired, sprinkle with confectioners' sugar or drizzle with honey.

About 2½ dozen

Honey Cookies *(Piernik)*

½ cup honey
½ cup sugar
2 eggs
½ teaspoon vanilla extract
3 cups all-purpose flour
1 teaspoon baking soda
½ teaspoon salt
½ teaspoon cinnamon
½ teaspoon ginger
½ teaspoon nutmeg
¼ teaspoon cloves
1 egg white, beaten
48 blanched almond halves (about)

1. Combine honey and sugar in a bowl; mix well. Beat in eggs and vanilla extract.
2. Blend flour, baking soda, salt, and spices. Stir into honey mixture. Knead to mix thoroughly; dough will be stiff.
3. Shape dough into a ball. Wrap in plastic wrap. Let stand 2 hours.
4. Roll dough on a floured surface to ¼-inch thickness. Cut into 2½-inch rounds or other shapes.
5. Brush top of each cookie with egg white. Press an almond onto center. Place on greased cookie sheets.
6. Bake at 375°F 8 to 10 minutes.
7. Cool on racks. Store in plastic bags for 8 to 10 days to mellow.

About 4 dozen

Called cookies, pastries, or dessert by purists, this sweet filled pastry is a favorite of many East Europeans. Although kolackys are generally thought of as Bohemian or Czech, Poles in some areas prize the varieties of fillings for these pastries almost as much as the varieties of toppings for mazurkas.

Kolacky

1 cup butter or margarine (at room temperature)
1 package (8 ounces) cream cheese (at room temperature)
¼ teaspoon vanilla extract
2¼ cups all-purpose flour
½ teaspoon salt
Thick jam or canned fruit filling, such as apricot or prune

1. Cream butter and cream cheese until fluffy. Beat in vanilla extract.
2. Combine flour and salt; add in fourths to butter mixture, blending well after each addition. Chill dough until easy to handle.
3. Roll dough to ⅜-inch thickness on a floured surface. Cut out 2-inch circles or other shapes. Place on ungreased baking sheets.
4. Make a "thumbprint" about ¼ inch deep in each cookie. Fill with jam.
5. Bake at 350°F 10 to 15 minutes, or until delicately browned on edges.

About 3½ dozen

Mazurkas *(Mazurek)*

1 cup sweet unsalted butter
¾ cup eggs, beaten
2 cups ground blanched almonds
1¾ cups all-purpose flour
1 cup sugar

1. Cream butter and eggs until fluffy.
2. Mix almonds, flour, and sugar. Add flour mixture, a small amount at a time, to the butter mixture. Beat or knead after each addition.
3. Pat or roll out dough in a greased 15×10×1-inch jelly-roll pan.
4. Bake at 350°F about 20 minutes, or until golden brown.
5. Spread jam over top. Cool for 5 minutes. Cut into 2-inch squares to serve.

About 3 dozen

Royal Mazurkas *(Mazurek Królewski)*

1 cup butter or margarine (room temperature)
1½ cups all-purpose flour
1 cup sugar
¼ teaspoon salt
6 egg yolks
¼ cup ground or finely chopped, blanched almonds
1 teaspoon grated orange or lemon peel (optional)

1. Cream butter until fluffy in a large mixing bowl.
2. Mix flour, sugar, and salt.
3. Alternately beat in 1 egg yolk and a sixth of flour mixture. Continue until all ingredients are well combined. Stir in almonds and orange peel. Mix well.
4. Roll or pat dough to fit a greased 15×10×1-inch jelly-roll pan.
5. Bake at 325°F 35 to 40 minutes, or until golden but not browned.
6. Cool in pan on rack 10 minutes. Cut in fourths. Remove from pan. Cool on rack.

About 3 dozen

Almond Mazurkas *(Mazurek Migdałowy)*

1 pound blanched almonds, ground (about 4 cups)
2 cups sugar
3 eggs
2 tablespoons lemon juice

1. Combine almonds and sugar; mix well.
2. Beat eggs with lemon juice just until foamy. Stir into almond mixture.
3. Pour batter into a well-greased 15×10×1-inch jelly-roll pan.
4. Bake at 250°F about 1 hour, or until golden.
5. Cut into 2-inch squares while still warm. Remove from pan.

About 3 dozen

Mazurkas with Fruit and Nut Topping

Mazurkas or Royal Mazurkas or Almond Mazurkas (see page 68)

Fruit Filling:
- ¾ cup raisins or currants
- ½ cup chopped dried apricots
- ¾ cup diced dried figs or dates
- ⅔ cup chopped candied lemon or orange peel
- ¾ cup chopped blanched almonds
- ½ cup chopped walnuts

Topping:
- 1 egg
- 1 egg white
- ½ cup confectioners' sugar
- ⅓ cup butter, melted
- 1 tablespoon lemon juice
- 1 teaspoon vanilla extract
- 2 ounces almonds, ground (about ¾ cup)
- 2 tablespoons bread crumbs

1. Prepare and bake mazurkas as directed. Do not cut into squares.
2. For fruit filling, combine apricots and raisins in a saucepan. Add **water.** Bring to boiling. Cover; remove from heat and let stand 10 minutes.
3. Drain raisins and apricots. Combine with other fruits and nuts. Spread evenly over mazurkas.
4. For topping, combine egg and egg white with confectioners' sugar. Beat at high speed until very thick and fluffy, about 7 minutes.
5. Gradually beat in melted butter, lemon juice, and vanilla extract. Fold in ground almonds and bread crumbs.
6. Spread egg mixture over fruit layer.
7. Bake at 350°F about 15 minutes, or until topping is golden but still moist.
8. Cool in pan on rack 5 minutes, then cut into squares.

About 3 dozen

Mazurkas with Chocolate Topping

Mazurkas or Royal Mazurkas or Almond Mazurkas (see page 68)
- 4 eggs
- 1 cup sugar
- ½ teaspoon vanilla extract
- 1 package (8 ounces) unsweetened chocolate, grated
- 1 tablespoon flour
- ½ teaspoon salt
- 1¼ cups chopped blanched almonds

1. Prepare and bake mazurkas as directed. Do not cut into squares.
2. Beat eggs with sugar and vanilla extract until fluffy. Add chocolate; beat until well mixed. Beat in flour, salt, and almonds.
3. Spread chocolate mixture over baked mazurkas.
4. Bake at 250°F 5 to 7 minutes, or until topping is set.
5. Cool. Cut into 2-inch squares.

About 3 dozen

Mazurkas with Apple Topping

Mazurkas or Royal Mazurkas or Almond Mazurkas (see page 68)
- 1 cup sugar
- ⅓ cup water
- 3 pounds apples, pared and thinly sliced
- 2 teaspoons grated lemon or orange peel
- ½ teaspoon salt (optional)
- 1½ cups finely chopped blanched almonds (optional)

1. Prepare and bake mazurkas as directed. Do not cut into squares.
2. Combine sugar and water in a large saucepan. Simmer 5 minutes. Add apples and lemon peel. Cook over medium heat until apples are soft, about 5 to 10 minutes; stir frequently to prevent sticking.
3. If desired, add salt and almonds. Cook and stir until apples are translucent on edges and mixture clings to the spoon. Remove from heat. Cool 15 to 20 minutes.
4. Spread apple filling over warm baked mazurkas. Cool completely. Cut into 2-inch squares.

About 3 dozen

Mazurkas with Lemon Icing

Mazurkas or Royal Mazurkas or
   Almond Mazurkas (see page
   68)
Lemon Icing:
   2 cups confectioners' sugar
   2 to 3 tablespoons lemon juice

1. Prepare and bake mazurkas as directed. Cool on a wire rack.
2. Meanwhile, mix confectioners' sugar with lemon juice until smooth.
3. Spread icing over mazurkas. Cut into 2-inch squares.

About 3 dozen

Black Bread Pudding *(Legumina Chlebowa)*

   6 eggs, separated
   ½ cup sugar
   ¼ teaspoon salt
   **1 cup fine dry bread crumbs made
      from black bread
      (pumpernickel, rye, or whole
      wheat bread)**
   ¾ teaspoon cinnamon
   ¼ teaspoon cloves
   **2 tablespoons melted butter
      Fine dry bread crumbs**

1. Beat egg yolks at high speed in a small bowl until thick. Gradually beat in sugar. Continue beating at high speed until mixture is very thick and piles softly.
2. Using clean beaters and a large bowl, beat egg whites with salt until stiff, not dry, peaks form.
3. Fold bread crumbs, cinnamon, and cloves into beaten yolks. Then fold in 1 tablespoon melted butter. Fold in egg whites.
4. Brush a 2-quart soufflé dish or deep casserole with remaining 1 tablespoon melted butter. Coat dish with bread crumbs.
5. Gently turn soufflé mixture into prepared dish.
6. Bake at 350°F 25 to 30 minutes, or until set near center.

About 6 servings

Chocolate Torte *(Tort Czekoladowy)*

   8 eggs, separated
   1¼ cups sugar
   ¾ cup all-purpose flour
   ¼ cup fine dry bread crumbs
   ¼ teaspoon salt
   **2 ounces (2 squares) semisweet
      chocolate, grated**
   **1½ teaspoons vanilla extract
      Filling (see below)
      Frosting (see below)**

1. Beat egg yolks until very thick and lemon-colored, about 5 minutes. Gradually beat in sugar.
2. Combine flour, bread crumbs, and salt. Add chocolate and mix thoroughly but lightly.
3. Add flour mixture to egg yolks and sugar in 4 portions, folding until well mixed after each addition.
4. With clean beaters, beat egg whites with vanilla extract until stiff, not dry, peaks are formed. Fold into flour mixture.
5. Turn into a well-greased 10-inch springform pan or deep, round layer cake pan.
6. Bake at 325°F 50 to 60 minutes. Remove from pan and cool completely.
7. Split cake in half.
8. Spread filling on bottom half. Replace top. Spread frosting over sides and top. Refrigerate 4 hours or longer for torte to mellow.

One 10-inch torte

Filling: Whip **½ cup whipping cream** until cream piles softly. Fold in **¼ cup ground almonds or walnuts** and **3 tablespoons sugar.**

Frosting: Melt **4 ounces (4 squares) unsweetened chocolate** and **3 tablespoons butter** together in a saucepan. Remove from heat. Stir in **1 tablespoon brandy.** Add **2 to 2½ cups confectioners' sugar** and **2 to 3 tablespoons milk or cream** until frosting is of spreading consistency.

Walnut Torte (Tort Orzechowy)

12 eggs, separated
1 cup sugar
½ pound finely ground walnuts
⅓ cup all-purpose flour
½ teaspoon salt
   Fine dry bread crumbs
2 to 3 tablespoons brandy or rum
   Filling
   Frosting
   Chopped walnuts

1. Beat egg yolks until thick and lemon-colored. Add sugar gradually, beating at high speed until mixture is very thick and piles softly.
2. Fold in ground walnuts and flour; mix thoroughly.
3. Beat egg whites with salt until stiff, but not dry, peaks form. Fold beaten egg whites into egg yolk mixture.
4. Generously grease two 10-inch cake layer pans or one 10-inch springform pan. Line with waxed paper. Grease paper. Coat with bread crumbs.
5. Turn batter into prepared pans.
6. Bake at 350°F about 25 minutes.
7. Remove layers from pans. Cool on racks 15 minutes. (Cut single, high cake, from springform pan, into 2 layers. Layers shrink slightly as they cool.) Sprinkle each layer with brandy. Cool completely.
8. Meanwhile, prepare filling and frosting.
9. Spread filling over 1 layer. Set second layer on top.
10. Spread frosting over top and sides of torte. Frosting is runny and will run down sides. Let stand 30 minutes. Pat chopped walnuts around sides of torte.
11. Refrigerate until ready to serve.

One 10-inch torte

Filling: Whip **1 cup whipping cream** until it is very thick and piles softly. Gradually beat in **¾ cup sugar**, then **½ teaspoon vanilla extract** and, if desired, **2 tablespoons brandy or rum**. Fold in **1 cup finely ground walnuts**, a small amount at a time, until blended.

About 2 cups

Frosting: Beat **1 egg** until thick and foamy. Beat in **2 tablespoons melted butter or margarine, 2 tablespoons brandy or rum, pinch salt,** and about **2½ cups sifted confectioners' sugar**. Add enough confectioners' sugar to make frosting of thin spreading consistency.

Plum Cake (Placek ze Śliwkami)

2⅓ cups all-purpose flour
2½ teaspoons baking powder
¾ teaspoon salt
1 cup sugar (reserve ¼ cup)
½ cup shortening
¾ cup milk
2 eggs
2 tablespoons fine dry bread crumbs
40 fresh plums (prune, Damson, or greengage), pitted and cut in half; or use 2 cans (30 ounces) whole purple plums, drained and pitted
3 tablespoons butter, cut in pieces
¼ teaspoon cloves

1. Combine flour, baking powder, salt, and ¾ cup sugar in a large mixing bowl. Add shortening, milk, and eggs. Beat at medium speed 4 minutes.
2. Grease bottom and sides of a 13×9×2-inch pan. Coat with bread crumbs.
3. Turn batter into prepared pan. Place plums on top, pushing one edge of each half down ¼ inch into batter. Dot with butter.
4. Combine remaining ¼ cup sugar and cloves; mix well. Sprinkle over plums.
5. Bake at 350°F about 40 minutes.
6. To serve, cut into pieces.

About 32

Apple Cake: Prepare Plum Cake as directed, substituting 4 large apples, pared and thinly sliced, for the plums.

Baba (Babka)

1 package active dry yeast
½ cup milk, scalded and cooled
½ cup sugar
2 cups all-purpose flour
½ cup butter (at room temperature)
4 eggs
½ teaspoon salt
½ teaspoon cinnamon
¼ teaspoon mace
1 tablespoon grated lemon peel
½ cup raisins, chopped almonds, or
    chopped candied fruits
    (optional)
    Lemon Icing (page 70) or honey

1. Dissolve yeast in milk 10 minutes. Add 1 tablespoon of the sugar and ½ cup of the flour; mix well. Cover. Let rise until doubled.
2. Cream butter, gradually adding remaining sugar. Beat until fluffy. Beat in 3 whole eggs, 1 at a time. Beat in 1 egg yolk; reserve remaining egg white.
3. Mix remaining flour with salt and spices. Beat into butter mixture. Stir in lemon peel and raisins.
4. Beat yeast mixture into butter mixture. Beat until batter is silky, about 10 to 15 minutes.
5. Turn into a well-greased and floured 10-inch baba or tube pan. Cover. Let rise until tripled in bulk, about 1½ hours.
6. Beat remaining egg white until foamy. Brush over top of baba.
7. Bake at 350°F about 40 minutes, until baba sounds hollow when tapped.
8. Cool on rack 10 minutes. Remove from pan. Drizzle with icing or brush with honey, if desired.

1 baba

Baba au Rhum: Prepare Baba as directed. Set in cake pan or shallow casserole. To prepare Rum Sauce: Boil **⅓ cup water, ⅓ cup sugar,** and **⅓ cup apricot jam** with **1 teaspoon lemon juice** 5 minutes. Add **½ cup rum.** Bring just to simmering. Pour over baba. With wooden pick, poke holes in baba. Continue pouring syrup over baba until all syrup is absorbed.

Filled Baba (Babki Śmietankowe)

Baba:
2 cups butter or margarine (at
    room temperature)
1 cup sugar
2 eggs
3 egg whites
2½ cups all-purpose flour
Custard:
3 egg yolks
¾ cup whipping cream
¾ cup sugar
¼ teaspoon salt

1. For baba, beat butter at high speed. Gradually add sugar, creaming until fluffy.
2. Beat in whole eggs and 2 egg whites. Stir in flour; mix well.
3. For custard, combine egg yolks, cream, sugar, and salt in the top of a double boiler or in a heavy saucepan. Cook and stir until custard is thickened. Set aside to cool a few minutes.
4. Generously grease muffin-pan wells; coat with fine dry bread crumbs. Line each with 1 tablespoon dough. Spoon in 2 tablespoons custard. Top with more dough.
5. Beat reserved egg white just until foamy. Brush top of each baba.
6. Bake at 350°F 20 to 25 minutes.

About 1½ dozen

Country Cheese Cake (Serowiec)

Dough:
- 1¾ cups all-purpose flour
- ½ cup confectioners' sugar
- ¾ teaspoon baking powder
- ¼ teaspoon salt
- ¼ cup butter or margarine
- 3 egg yolks
- 3 tablespoons dairy sour cream

Filling:
- 4 eggs
- 1 egg white
- ¾ cup sugar
- 1½ pounds farmer or pot cheese or ricotta
- ½ cup dairy sour cream
- 2 tablespoons grated orange peel
- 1 teaspoon vanilla extract

1. For dough, combine flour, sugar, baking powder, and salt in a bowl. With pastry blender, cut butter into flour mixture until coarse and crumbly.
2. Beat egg yolks into sour cream. Stir into flour mixture. Knead in bowl until dough is well mixed and holds its shape.
3. Refrigerate dough until easy to roll out, at least 1 hour.
4. Roll out dough on a floured surface to fit a 13×9×2-inch pan, about a 15×11-inch rectangle.
5. Line bottom of pan, fitting dough so it comes about ⅔ of the way up sides of pan.
6. For filling, beat eggs and egg white at high speed of electric mixer until thick. Gradually add sugar, beating at high speed until stiff, not dry, peaks form.
7. Press cheese through a sieve. Fold into beaten egg mixture. Add remaining ingredients. Mix gently but thoroughly. Turn filling into dough-lined pan.
8. Bake at 350°F about 40 minutes, or until set.
9. Cool before cutting into squares.

About 16 servings

Apples in Blankets (Jabłuszka w Cieście)

- 1 pound apples, pared and cored
- 2 eggs
- ⅓ cup sugar
- Dash salt
- 1¼ cups all-purpose flour
- ⅓ cup dairy sour cream
- ¼ cup buttermilk
- Fat for deep frying heated to 365°F
- Confectioners' sugar
- Nutmeg or cinnamon (optional)

1. Slice apples crosswise to make rings about ⅜ inch thick.
2. Beat eggs with sugar until thick and foamy. Add salt. Beat in small amounts of flour alternately with sour cream and buttermilk. Beat until batter is well mixed.
3. Coat apple slices with batter. Fry in hot fat until golden.
4. Drain on paper towels. Sprinkle with confectioners' sugar. Add a dash of nutmeg or cinnamon, if desired.

About 14

Raspberry Syrup (Sok Malinowy)

- 2 cups sugar
- ½ cup water
- 2 cups fresh or frozen raspberries

1. Combine sugar and water in a saucepan.
2. Bring to boiling; add raspberries. Boil 3 minutes. Remove from heat.
3. Line a strainer or colander with cheesecloth. Set over a bowl. Turn cooked berries into cloth-lined strainer. Let drain 2 hours.
4. Discard seeds and pulp. Return juice to saucepan. Boil about 12 minutes, or until reduced to half the original amount. Skim off foam.
5. Pour into a clean jar. Cover. Store in refrigerator. Serve with fruit compote, fresh fruits, or as a sauce for cake.

About 2 cups

Pear Compote (Kompot z Gruszek)

8 pears or 4 cups pitted dark sweet cherries
1½ cups wine
⅔ cup sugar
⅓ cup red currant jelly
½ teaspoon vanilla extract or 1 tablespoon lemon juice
4 whole cloves
1 stick cinnamon

1. Pare pears, leaving whole with stems attached.
2. Combine wine, and remaining ingredients. Bring to boiling.
3. Add pears. Simmer until pears are transparent on the edges, about 45 minutes. (Boil cherries 2 minutes.)
4. Remove fruit to serving dish.
5. Boil syrup until very thick, about 20 minutes. Pour over fruit.
6. Chill. Serve with whipped cream or soft dessert cheese, if desired.

8 servings

Berry Compote (Kompot z Malin lub Truskawek)

1 pint strawberries or raspberries
1 cup water
½ cup sugar
½ cup white dessert wine

1. Wash and hull berries. Put into a glass bowl.
2. Boil water with sugar 5 minutes. Pour over berries and add wine. Let stand 2 hours before serving. Chill, if desired.

4 servings

Fruit Compote in Spirits (Kompot w Spirytusie)

2 pounds ripe peaches, pears, or apricots
1⅓ cups water
2 cups sugar
¾ cup white rum, vodka, or grain alcohol

1. Dip whole fruit, 1 piece at a time, in boiling water for a few seconds to loosen skin. Pull off skin; leave fruit whole.
2. Combine water with sugar in a saucepan. Boil 5 minutes.
3. Add fruits and simmer 3 minutes for small fruit; 5 minutes for large fruit.
4. Remove from heat. Skim off foam. Let stand overnight.
5. Remove fruit from syrup. Boil syrup 1 minute. Skim off foam. Pour syrup over fruit. Let stand overnight.
6. Remove fruits from syrup. Place in sterilized jars. Bring syrup to boiling; skim off foam. Add rum and pour over fruit. Seal.
7. Store in a cool, dry place at least 1 week before using.

6 to 8 servings

Pear and Apple Compote
(Kompot z Gruszek i Jabłek)

2 cups water
⅔ cup sugar
6 pears, pared, cored, quartered
2 apples, pared, cored, quartered
8 whole cloves
½ cup currant or gooseberry jelly

1. Bring water with sugar to boiling in a large saucepan. Boil 5 minutes.
2. Add fruits and cloves. Simmer until fruits are tender, about 7 to 10 minutes.
3. Remove fruits and place in a serving bowl. Discard cloves. Boil syrup until only 1 cup remains.
4. Blend syrup into jelly. Return to saucepan. Bring just to boiling. Pour over fruits. Let stand 1 hour before serving, or chill.

6 to 8 servings

EASTER

Easter is one of the happiest days of the year in Poland. The Poles have strictly observed the forty-day penitential season of Lent and by the time Easter comes they are more than ready for a feast. The larks have returned, the storks are on the rooftops again, and flowers have begun to bloom. On Good Friday night hard-cooked eggs have been colored and decorated with traditional designs; on Easter Saturday baskets filled

with salt, hard-cooked eggs, butter, and other foods have been brought to church for the priest to bless. Everything is ready. The feasting begins with the favorite breakfast of the year, called *Święcone.* Then the table is set with the best family linen and decorated with branches of pussy willow and garlands of green leaves. Set in the center is the Paschal lamb, made of sugar or butter or, at times, baba dough. The lamb often holds a Polish flag as a standard of victory over death.

Then the buffet is laid out. Succulent cold meats—roast beef, baked ham, sausage, roast veal, roast turkey, roast goose—surround the highlight of the feast: a roast suckling pig.

The meats are supported by hard-cooked eggs, sauces, and relishes, especially the traditional Easter relish of beets and horseradish, *ćwikła.* On the side is set a steaming tureen of *barszcz.*

Pastries and sweets also abound on the Easter table, with special rich babas and a cheese cake with raisins always featured. Then, as a final, glorious touch, honey-flavored, spiced vodka *(krupnik)* and other sweet liqueurs sparkle in elegant decanters.

Once everything is prepared, open house is declared and all invited. The father or mother of the family (depending on the region of the country) greets each guest with a wedge of hard-cooked egg and wishes him or her good health and happiness.

As might be expected, there is quite a bit of meat left over from the Easter buffet. This is easily taken care of on Easter

Monday in that most marvelous of all stews—*bigos* or hunter's stew. Easter Monday is usually a holiday and, because of the *bigos*, it too is a feast.

All in all, never has the fasting of Lent been forgotten in more magnificent style.

EASTER BUFFET

Hard-Cooked Eggs
Clear Borscht (page 26)
Roast Leg of Lamb (page 48)
Roast Loin of Pork (page 48)
Polish Sausage (page 78)
Baked Ham
Roast Beef
Roasted Veal (page 79)

Roast Turkey with Anchovies (page 55)
Roast Goose
Roast Suckling Pig (page 79)
Red Beets with Horseradish (page 79)
Easter Baba (page 80)
Grandmother's Cheese Cake (page 81)
Mazurkas (pages 68–70)
Krupnik (Fire Vodka) (page 84)

Egg Crowns

6 hard-cooked eggs, peeled and sliced
30 small rounds of buttered bread
1 package (3 ounces) cream cheese (at room temperature)
2 tablespoons mayonnaise
1 teaspoon prepared mustard
½ teaspoon salt
½ teaspoon vinegar
1 jar (2 ounces) pimento strips, drained
Watercress

1. Remove yolks from eggs; put into a sieve over a bowl. Place rings of white on buttered bread.
2. Sieve egg yolks and ends of whites.
3. Mix sieved eggs, cream cheese, mayonnaise, mustard, salt, and vinegar. Beat until smooth.
4. With 2 spoons or pastry tube and star tip, fill each egg white ring with yolk mixture. Garnish with pimento strips and watercress.

30 canapés

Eggs with Anchovies *(Jajka ze Sardelkami)*

4 hard-cooked eggs
Lettuce leaves
16 anchovy fillets
2 tablespoons mayonnaise
1 dill pickle, sliced
1 tomato, sliced

1. Peel the eggs; cut in halves.
2. Arrange eggs, yolks up, on a dish covered with lettuce leaves.
3. Place 2 anchovy fillets over each egg to form an "X."
4. Garnish with mayonnaise, pickle, and tomato slices.

8 egg halves

Veal Pâté *(Pasztet z Cielęciny)*

1 pound pork liver, cut up
2 cups milk
6 dried mushrooms or 8 ounces fresh mushrooms
1 large onion, quartered
1 bay leaf
5 peppercorns
1 pound veal, cut up
1 pound sliced bacon
2 cups chicken bouillon
3 slices white bread
3 eggs
½ teaspoon nutmeg
Pinch allspice
Salt and pepper

1. Soak liver in milk 1 hour. Drain; discard milk.
2. Scrub mushrooms gently with a brush. Put dried mushrooms into a large saucepan. Add onion, bay leaf, peppercorns, veal, bacon, and bouillon; simmer 1 hour. Add the liver and fresh mushrooms (if used). Simmer 30 minutes longer.
3. Strain off the bouillon and soak bread in it.
4. Combine mushrooms, onion, veal, ¾ of the bacon, liver, and bread. Grind twice.
5. Combine eggs with ground mixture, season with nutmeg, allspice, and salt and pepper to taste. Mix very well.
6. Line a 9×5×3-inch pan with the remaining bacon. Pack with the meat mixture. Cover with foil.
7. Bake at 350°F 1 hour. Cool.
8. Serve with Horseradish Sauce (page 88), or Red Beets with Horseradish (page 79).

About 12 servings

Turkey Pâté: Follow recipe for Veal Pâté, using **turkey** or **chicken livers** instead of pork liver and **turkey meat** instead of veal. Omit allspice.

Easter Soup (Żurek Wielkanocny)

2 cups rolled oats
2 cups warm water
   Crust of sour rye bread
1½ pounds Polish sausage
   (kiełbasa)
1½ quarts water
1 tablespoon prepared horseradish
1 teaspoon brown sugar
1 teaspoon salt
¼ teaspoon pepper

1. Mix oats and warm water. Add bread crust. Let stand until mixture sours, at least 24 hours. Strain; reserve liquid.
2. Cook sausage in 1½ quarts water 1 hour. Remove sausage. Skim off fat. Combine skimmed broth and oatmeal liquid.
3. Add horseradish, brown sugar, salt, and pepper. Slice sausage; add to broth. Bring just to boiling.
4. Serve hot with **boiled potatoes** and **hard-cooked eggs.**

About 4 servings

Polish Sausage (Kiełbasa)

1½ pounds lean boneless pork
½ pound boneless veal
1 teaspoon salt
¼ teaspoon pepper
1 clove garlic, crushed
1 tablespoon mustard seed
¼ cup crushed ice
   Casing

1. Cut meat into small chunks. Grind meat with seasonings and ice; mix well.
2. Stuff meat mixture into casing.
3. Smoke in a smoker, following manufacturer's directions. Or, place sausage in a casserole; cover with water. Bake at 350°F until water is absorbed, about 1½ hours. Roast 10 minutes.

About 2 pounds

Ham in Rye Crust

Dough:
1 package active dry yeast
½ cup warm water
⅓ cup caraway seed
¾ cup water
2 tablespoons molasses
3 cups rye flour (about)
Topping for ham:
½ cup firmly packed brown sugar
1 teaspoon dry mustard
¼ teaspoon cloves

1 canned fully cooked ham
   (5 pounds)

1. For dough, dissolve yeast in ½ cup warm water and add caraway seed; let stand 10 minutes.
2. Stir in ¾ cup water, molasses, and half of the flour.
3. Turn out dough onto floured surface. Knead in remaining flour to make a stiff dough. Cover with plastic wrap. Let rest 20 minutes.
4. Mix brown sugar with mustard and cloves.
5. Remove gelatin and wipe ham with paper towels.
6. Roll out dough on a floured surface to form a 28×10-inch rectangle.
7. Sprinkle about 1 tablespoon brown sugar mixture in center of dough. Place ham on sugar mixture. Sprinkle remaining sugar mixture over top of ham.
8. Fold dough over top of ham, cutting out corners to fit with only one layer of dough. Pinch edges to seal.
9. Set dough-wrapped ham on rack in pan lined with foil.
10. Roast at 350°F 1½ to 1¾ hours, or until meat thermometer reaches 140°F. Remove from oven; let rest 10 minutes.
11. To serve, remove crust and discard. Slice ham.

12 to 15 servings

Roasted Veal *(Pieczeń Cielęca)*

1 veal leg round roast or shoulder
    arm roast (4 to 5 pounds)
Boiling water
3 tablespoons lemon juice
1 tablespoon salt
1 teaspoon pepper
½ cup butter, melted
Flour for dusting

1. Dip meat quickly in boiling water; drain well.
2. Mix lemon juice, salt, and pepper. Spread over surface of meat.
3. Place meat on a spit or rack in a roasting pan.
4. Roast at 400°F 20 minutes. Reduce heat to 325°F. Roast 55 minutes.
5. Baste with melted butter. Sprinkle flour over top. Roast 10 minutes longer, or until done as desired.

6 to 8 servings

Roast Suckling Pig *(Prosię Pieczone)*

1 suckling pig, about 25 to 30
    pounds
Salt and pepper
1½ pounds stale bread, diced
1½ cups milk
2 eggs
2 apples, sliced
2 onions, diced
⅓ cup chopped parsley
1 potato
Melted lard or salad oil
1 small whole apple
Parsley sprigs or small fruits
    and leaves

1. Wipe pig, inside and out, with a clean damp cloth. Sprinkle entire cavity with salt and pepper. If necessary to make pig fit into pan (and oven) cut crosswise in half just behind shoulders.
2. Put bread into a large mixing bowl. Add milk and let soak 20 minutes. Add eggs, sliced apples, onion, and parsley; mix well.
3. Spoon stuffing into cavity of pig. (There will not be enough stuffing to entirely fill cavity.)
4. Use metal skewers to hold cavity closed and lace with string.
5. Set pig belly side down in roasting pan. Tuck feet under body. Cover tail, snout, and ears with foil. Place whole potato in mouth.
6. Roast at 375°F 8 to 10 hours. Baste frequently with melted lard. When pig is done, juices run golden and skin is a crackling, translucent, golden-chocolate brown.
7. Set pig on platter. Remove potato from mouth; replace with apple. Make a wreath of parsley sprigs for neck or to cover joint behind shoulders.

About 25 servings

Red Beets with Horseradish *(Ćwikła)*

3 cups cooked or canned red beets,
    drained and coarsely chopped
6 ounces prepared cream-style
    horseradish
1 tablespoon brown sugar
1 teaspoon vinegar
¼ teaspoon salt

1. Combine all ingredients. Cover; refrigerate 3 days.
2. Serve with cold meats.

About 3 cups

Easter Baba (Babka Wielkanocna)

1 cup milk
3⅓ cups all-purpose flour
2 packages active dry yeast
¼ cup lukewarm water
⅔ cup sugar
2 teaspoons salt
15 egg yolks
1 teaspoon vanilla extract
¼ teaspoon almond extract
½ cup melted butter
¾ cup mixed chopped candied citron and orange and lemon peel
½ cup chopped almonds
⅓ cup raisins
Blanched almond halves
Fine dry bread crumbs

1. Scald milk; pour into a large bowl. Slowly add ¾ cup flour to hot milk and beat thoroughly. Cool.
2. Dissolve yeast in lukewarm water 5 minutes; add 1 tablespoon of the sugar. Let stand 5 minutes. Add to cooled milk mixture; beat well.
3. Cover; let rise until doubled in bulk.
4. Add salt to egg yolks. Beat until thick and lemon-colored, about 5 minutes. Add remaining sugar and extracts; continue beating. Combine egg mixture with milk mixture, beating thoroughly. Add remaining flour; mix well.
5. Knead 10 minutes in bowl. Add butter and continue kneading 10 more minutes, or until dough leaves the fingers. Add candied peel, almonds, and raisins; knead to mix well.
6. Let rise until doubled in bulk. Punch down and let rise again.
7. Generously grease a 12-inch fluted tube pan or turban mold. Press almond halves around sides and bottom of pan. Coat with bread crumbs.
8. Punch down dough and put into prepared pan. Dough should fill a third of pan. Let rise 1 hour, or until dough fills pan.
9. Bake at 350°F about 50 minutes, or until hollow sounding when tapped on top.

1 large loaf

Baba with Raisins (Babka z Rodzynkami)

1 cup butter or margarine (at room temperature)
1½ cups confectioners' sugar
4 eggs, separated
¼ cup orange juice
4 teaspoons lemon juice
1 tablespoon grated orange or lemon peel
4 teaspoons baking powder
1½ cups all-purpose flour
1 cup cornstarch
⅓ cup confectioners' sugar
½ teaspoon salt
½ cup raisins
Fine dry bread crumbs
1 tablespoon whipping cream (optional)

1. Cream butter. Gradually add 1½ cups confectioners' sugar, beating at high speed of electric mixer. Beat in egg yolks, one at a time. Beat in orange juice, lemon juice, and orange peel.
2. Mix flour, cornstarch, and ⅓ cup confectioners' sugar.
3. With clean beaters, beat egg whites with salt until stiff, not dry, peaks form.
4. Fold half the flour mixture into the butter mixture. Fold in egg whites.
5. Add raisins to remaining flour mixture; mix well. Fold into batter.
6. Generously grease an 11-cup ring mold or baba pan. Coat with bread crumbs.
7. Turn batter into prepared pan. Brush top with cream.
8. Bake at 350°F about 40 minutes.

1 baba

Grandmother's Cheesecake (foreground), **81**, and **Baba**, **80**, mark Easter, as do painted eggs and hand-worked tablecloths.

Grandmother's Cheese Cake *(Sernik Babci)*

Dough:
- 1¼ cups all-purpose flour
- ¾ teaspoon baking powder
- ¼ teaspoon salt
- ¼ cup butter or margarine
- 1 egg
- 3 tablespoons dairy sour cream
- ⅓ cup confectioners' sugar

Filling:
- 6 eggs
- 2 cups confectioners' sugar
- 1½ teaspoons vanilla extract
- 1 pound farmer cheese or ricotta
- ⅔ cup melted butter
- 1½ cups unseasoned mashed potatoes
- 2 teaspoons baking powder
- ½ teaspoon nutmeg
- ½ teaspoon salt
- ¼ cup grated orange or lemon peel

1. For dough, combine flour, baking powder, and salt in a bowl. Cut in butter with a pastry blender.
2. Beat egg into sour cream. Stir into flour mixture. Stir in sugar. Knead dough until well mixed and smooth.
3. Roll dough on a floured surface into a rectangle. Line a 13×9×2-inch pan with dough, and bring dough part way up sides.
4. For filling, separate 1 egg and reserve the white. Beat remaining yolk and whole eggs with the sugar 5 minutes at high speed of electric mixer. Add vanilla extract. Beat at high speed until mixture piles softly.
5. Press cheese through a sieve. Blend cheese with butter; add potatoes, baking powder, nutmeg, and salt. Stir in orange peel. Fold into egg mixture. Turn into prepared crust in pan.
6. Bake at 350°F about 45 minutes, or until set. Cool.
7. Cool well before cutting.

About 32 pieces

Lamb Cake

- 2 cups sifted cake flour
- ¾ teaspoon baking powder
- ¼ teaspoon salt
- ¼ teaspoon mace
- 1 cup butter or margarine
- 1 cup plus 2 tablespoons sugar
- 2 teaspoons grated lemon peel
- 1½ teaspoons vanilla extract
- ½ teaspoon almond extract
- 4 eggs
- 1 tablespoon flour
- 2 tablespoons shortening
  Seven-Minute Frosting (see recipe)
  Shredded coconut

1. Sift together cake flour, baking powder, salt, and mace.
2. Cream butter. Gradually add sugar, creaming until fluffy. Add lemon peel and extracts.
3. Alternately beat in eggs and flour mixture.
4. Blend 1 tablespoon flour into shortening. Brush over both inside sections of a lamb mold.
5. Turn batter into face side of mold, filling it level. Spoon a small amount of batter into back side of mold, filling ears. Close and lock mold. Set on baking sheet.
6. Bake at 375°F 50 to 55 minutes.
7. Set mold on wire rack to cool 5 minutes. Remove back side. Cool 5 minutes longer. Turn out on rack to cool completely.
8. Frost with Seven-Minute Frosting. Coat with coconut.

1 lamb cake

Seven-Minute Frosting

- 1½ cups sugar
- ⅓ cup water
- 1 tablespoon light corn syrup
- ⅛ teaspoon salt
- 2 egg whites (unbeaten)
- ½ teaspoon vanilla extract

1. Combine sugar, water, corn syrup, salt, and egg whites in the top of a double boiler. Set over boiling water and beat at high speed 7 to 10 minutes, or until stiff peaks form when beater is lifted.
2. Remove from heat. Beat in vanilla extract.

About 5 cups

The Polish tradition calling for twelve courses at Christmas Eve dinner is often replaced today by serving the **Twelve-Fruit Compote, 93.**

Easter Cheese Cake (Sernik Wielkanocny)

**Dough for Grandmother's
Cheese Cake (page 81) or
Country Cheese Cake (page
73)**

Cheese Filling:

- 6 eggs
- 2¼ cups confectioners' sugar
- 1½ pounds farmer cheese or ricotta
- ⅔ cup butter or margarine (at room temperature)
- ½ teaspoon salt
- 1½ teaspoons vanilla extract
- 2 teaspoons grated lemon peel
- ¼ cup finely chopped candied orange peel
- ⅓ cup raisins

Spread:

- ¾ cup thick raspberry jam or strawberry preserves

1. Prepare dough for crust; line pan.
2. Beat eggs at high speed until thickened. Slowly beat in sugar, beating until mixture piles softly.
3. Press cheese through a sieve. Beat cheese with butter, salt, vanilla extract, and lemon peel.
4. Fold eggs into cheese mixture. Stir in orange peel and raisins.
5. Spread jam over bottom of prepared crust in pan.
6. Turn cheese mixture into pan.
7. Bake at 325°F 45 minutes to 1 hour or until a knife inserted near center comes out clean.
8. Cool well before cutting.

32 pieces

This is an old, traditional Easter delicacy from the eastern regions of Poland.

Cheese Pascha from Lwow (Pascha ze Lwowa)

- 1 whole egg
- 4 egg yolks
- 2⅔ cups sugar
- 1 cup whipping cream
- 1 cup raisins or currants
- 2 pounds white farmer cheese
- ½ pound unsalted sweet butter
- 1 tablespoon vanilla extract
- 1 cup chopped blanched almonds
- 2 tablespoons grated orange peel

1. Beat whole egg and egg yolks with sugar until thick and creamy. Add half of cream. Turn into a saucepan. Heat almost to the boiling point, stirring constantly; do not boil. Remove from heat. Add raisins; cover.
2. Combine the rest of the cream, the cheese, butter, and vanilla extract in a large electric blender. Blend until smooth.
3. Turn cheese mixture into a bowl. Fold in the egg mixture. Add almonds and orange peel.
4. Refrigerate 4 hours. Place in a double thickness of cheesecloth. Hang over a bowl in a cold place; let drain 24 hours. Chill. Garnish with **nuts** and **candied fruits** as desired. Serve cold. Cut small slices.

16 to 20 servings

Cross Cake

1 cup butter or margarine
1½ cups sugar
4 eggs
1 teaspoon vanilla extract
½ teaspoon salt
4 cups sifted cake flour
4 teaspoons baking powder
1⅓ cups milk
Basic Butter Frosting (see recipe)
Butter Cream Decorating Frosting (see recipe)

1. Beat butter until softened. Gradually add sugar, creaming until fluffy. Add eggs, 1 at a time, beating thoroughly after each. Add vanilla extract and salt; beat well.
2. Mix flour with baking powder; alternately add with milk to creamed mixture, beating thoroughly after each addition.
3. Turn into a greased and floured 13×9×2-inch baking pan and spread evenly to edges.
4. Bake at 350°F about 45 minutes, or until top springs back when lightly touched.
5. Cool in pan on rack 5 minutes. Turn out onto rack; cool completely.
6. Cut out 3-inch squares from the two top corners of cake.
7. Cut out 6×2-inch rectangles from the two corners of the lower section of cake, leaving the cake in the form of a cross. Frost and decorate as desired.

1 cross cake

Basic Butter Frosting

6 tablespoons butter or margarine
1½ teaspoons vanilla extract
3 cups confectioners' sugar
1½ tablespoons milk or cream

1. Cream butter with vanilla extract. Add confectioners' sugar gradually, beating thoroughly after each addition.
2. Stir in milk and beat until frosting is of spreading consistency.

About 2 cups

Lemon Butter Frosting: Follow recipe for Basic Butter Frosting. Substitute **lemon juice** for milk and add **1½ teaspoons grated lemon peel.** If desired, add a few drops yellow food coloring.

Orange Butter Frosting: Follow recipe for Basic Butter Frosting. Substitute **1½ teaspoons grated orange peel** for the vanilla extract and **1½ to 2½ tablespoons orange juice** for the milk. If a deeper orange color is desired, mix 4 drops red food coloring and 3 drops yellow food coloring with orange juice.

Butter Cream Decorating Frosting

½ cup all-purpose shortening
¼ cup butter or margarine
1 teaspoon lemon extract
3 cups sifted confectioners' sugar

Beat shortening, margarine, and lemon extract together in an electric mixer bowl. Gradually beat in confectioners' sugar until frosting will hold the shape of a tube design.

About 2 cups

Excellent Warsaw Paczki
(Wyborne Warszawskie Pączki)

12 egg yolks
1 teaspoon salt
2 packages active dry yeast
¼ cup warm water
⅓ cup butter or margarine (at room temperature)
½ cup sugar
4½ cups all-purpose flour
3 tablespoons rum or brandy
1 cup whipping cream, scalded
1½ cups very thick jam or preserves (optional)
Fat for deep frying heated to 365°F

1. Beat egg yolks with salt in a small mixer bowl at high speed of electric mixer until mixture is thick and piles softly, about 7 minutes.
2. Soften yeast in warm water in a large bowl.
3. Cream butter; add sugar gradually, creaming until fluffy. Beat into softened yeast.
4. Stir one fourth of flour into yeast mixture. Add rum and half the cream. Beat in another one fourth of the flour. Stir in remaining cream. Beat in half the remaining flour. Then beat in egg yolks. Beat 2 minutes. Gradually beat in remaining flour until dough blisters.
5. Cover bowl with plastic wrap. Set in a warm place to rise. When doubled in bulk, punch down. Cover; let dough rise again until doubled. Punch down.
6. Roll dough on a floured surface to about ¾-inch thickness. Cut out 3-inch rounds. Use a regular doughnut cutter for plain. Use a biscuit cutter for filled doughnuts.
7. To fill doughnuts, place 1 teaspoonful of jam in center of half the rounds. Brush edges of rounds with water. Top with remaining rounds. Seal edges.
8. Cover doughnuts on floured surface. Let rise until doubled in bulk, about 20 minutes.
9. Fry doughnuts in hot fat until golden brown on both sides. Drain on absorbent paper. Sprinkle with cinnamon sugar, if desired.

About 3 dozen

Fire Vodka (Krupnik)

1½ cups honey
⅔ cup water
1 teaspoon vanilla extract or 1 vanilla bean
¼ teaspoon nutmeg
8 sticks cinnamon
2 whole cloves
3 strips lemon peel (2 inches each)
1 bottle (4/5 quart) vodka

1. Combine honey with water, vanilla, spices, and lemon peel in a large saucepan. Bring to boiling; cover. Simmer 5 minutes.
2. Add vodka. Remove from heat. Serve hot or cooled.

About 1 quart

CHRISTMAS

The Christmas season in Poland follows religious tradition, beginning four Sundays before Christmas with a period of preparation called Advent and continuing until Candlemas Day (February 2). During this period there are days of special festivity singled out: *St. Andrew's Eve* (November 29), when young girls drip candlewax on water to foretell whether they will marry and to what kind of a husband; *St. Nicholas*

Day (December 6) when a jolly man dressed like a bishop walks through the streets passing out pierniki to the children who shout "*Już idzie*" (he comes); *New Year's Eve*, with its late buffet and champagne at midnight; *Epiphany*, when the coming of the wise men (Kaspar, Melchior, and Baltazar) is remembered by inscribing the initials KMB over the door; and *Candlemas Day,* when candles are blessed in the church and then reserved for use during storms and at times of sickness and death.

The reason for all the celebration is Christ's birth and, naturally, Christmas Eve and Christmas Day are the days of most celebration. Christmas trees and crèches are found in homes, churches, and city squares. In the city, trees are placed on tables or on the floor; in the country they are hung from the ceiling. In either case they are decorated with lights, apples, nuts, candies, and toys. Also hung from the ceiling are *pająki,* a decoration similar to a spider web, and a *dożynki,* a colorful harvest wreath embellished with flowers and stars. Straw is placed under the white tablecloth as a reminder of the stable in which Christ was born. Gifts are given on Christmas Eve. The young children believe they were brought by angels (St. Nicholas had already distributed his gifts on December 6).

One of the most memorable meals of the year is eaten after sundown on Christmas Eve *(Wigilia)*. Although it is meatless (Advent, the season of penance, continues until midnight), it is still festive and delicious. In the past, there were twelve main dishes; this is often replaced today by a twelve-fruit compote. In some areas of Poland only an odd

number of courses can be served and there must be an even number of people at the table. An empty place is normally left for any stranger who might come by.

Christmas Day itself is usually spent visiting relatives and friends. In most homes little or no cooking is done on this day.

CHRISTMAS EVE DINNER

Pickled Beets (page 89)

Noodles with Poppy Seed and Raisins (page 90)

Poppy Seed Rolls (page 92)

Christmas Bread (page 92)

Light Fruitcake from Warsaw (page 93)

Twelve-Fruit Compote (page 93)

Pickled Herring in Sour Cream (page 87)

Borscht without Meat (page 87)

Cheese and Sauerkraut Filled Pierogi (page 36)

Northern Pike Polish Style (page 46)

Fish in Horseradish Sauce (page 88)

Stewed Sauerkraut with Mushrooms (page 89)

Pickled Herring in Sour Cream
(Śledzie Marynowane w Śmietanie)

6 pickled herring, drained
1 large onion, peeled and chopped
6 hard-cooked eggs, peeled and chopped
1 apple, cored and chopped
1 teaspoon lemon juice
1 cup dairy sour cream
1 clove garlic, crushed (optional)
¼ teaspoon salt
⅛ teaspoon pepper
2 tablespoons chopped fresh dill or parsley

1. Cut herring into small cubes. Mix herring with onion, eggs, apple, and lemon juice.
2. Combine sour cream, garlic (if desired), salt, and pepper; add to herring mixture and mix well. Sprinkle with dill.
3. Serve with **dark bread.**

4 to 6 servings

Borscht without Meat (Barszcz Postny)

7 medium beets (about 1½ pounds)
2 medium potatoes (about ½ pound) (optional)
½ cup chopped parsley root or 2 tablespoons dried parsley flakes
⅓ cup chopped celery leaves
4 dried mushrooms or 4 fresh mushrooms
1 clove garlic, crushed (optional)
2 quarts water
1½ cups Beet Kvas (see page 19)
3 beef bouillon cubes or 1 tablespoon concentrated meat extract
2 teaspoons salt
1 tablespoon sugar
Dairy sour cream (optional)

1. Pare beets and potatoes, then dice them.
2. Combine all ingredients in a 6-quart kettle. Bring to boiling. Reduce heat. Cover and cook over medium heat until vegetables are tender, 30 to 40 minutes.
3. Remove vegetables and force through a sieve or purée in an electric blender. Return purée to kettle. (This is optional and may be omitted.)
4. Various ingredients may be added to soup: prepared horseradish, lemon juice or vinegar, dill, more salt and sugar, pepper, chunks of rye bread, or filled pastries such as pierogi. Sometimes sliced or chopped hard-cooked eggs, beet tops, and baked beans are added. Simmer just long enough to heat thoroughly.
5. Serve in large bowls with dollops of sour cream, if desired.

About 5 quarts

Almond Soup (Zupa Migdałowa)

5 cups milk
½ pound blanched almonds, ground twice
5 bitter almonds (optional)
1 teaspoon almond extract
2 cups cooked rice
⅓ cup sugar
¼ cup raisins or currants

1. Heat milk just to simmering in a large saucepan.
2. Add all the ingredients; stir until well mixed. Cook over low heat 3 to 5 minutes.
3. Serve hot as is traditional for Christmas, or chill before serving.

About 2 quarts

Fish in Horseradish Sauce
(Ryba w Sosie Chrzanowym)

2 carrots
2 stalks celery (optional)
1 parsley root
1 onion, quartered
1 bay leaf
5 peppercorns
2 teaspoons salt
1½ quarts water
2 pounds carp, sole, or pike fillets

Horseradish Sauce:
3 tablespoons butter or margarine
3 tablespoons flour
¾ cup prepared cream-style horseradish
½ teaspoon sugar
¼ teaspoon salt
⅔ cup dairy sour cream
2 hard-cooked eggs, peeled and sieved

Garnish:
Shredded lettuce

1. Combine vegetables, dry seasonings, and water in a saucepot. Bring to boiling; simmer 20 minutes. Strain.
2. Cook fish in the strained vegetable stock 6 to 10 minutes, or until fish flakes easily.
3. Remove fish from stock. Arrange on serving platter and cover with plastic wrap. Chill.
4. Strain fish stock and reserve ¾ cup for horseradish sauce; cool.
5. For horseradish sauce, melt butter in a saucepan; blend in flour until smooth.
6. Add the cooked fish stock gradually, stirring constantly. Cook and stir until the sauce boils and becomes thick and smooth.
7. Remove from heat. Stir in horseradish, sugar, salt, sour cream, and eggs. Cool 15 minutes.
8. Pour the horseradish sauce over chilled fish. Garnish with shredded lettuce.

About 6 servings

Sauerkraut with Dried Peas
(for Christmas Eve) (Kapustą z Grochem)

1 cup dried split green or yellow peas, rinsed
2⅔ cups boiling water
1 quart sauerkraut, rinsed and drained
½ cup chopped mushrooms
3 cups water
Salt and pepper
1 can (2 ounces) anchovies, drained

1. Combine peas and 2⅔ cups boiling water in a saucepan. Bring to boiling and boil 2 minutes. Remove from heat. Cover and let soak 30 minutes. Bring to boiling; simmer 20 minutes.
2. Cover sauerkraut and mushrooms with 3 cups water in a saucepan; cover and cook 1 hour.
3. Add cooked peas to sauerkraut mixture. Season to taste with salt and pepper; mix well. Turn into a buttered baking dish. Top with anchovies. Cover.
4. Bake at 325°F 30 minutes.

4 to 6 servings

Sauerkraut with Dried Peas (for nonfast days): Prepare Sauerkraut with Dried Peas; omit anchovies and baking. Fry **1 onion, chopped,** with **½ pound salt pork or bacon,** chopped, until lightly browned. Blend in **2 tablespoons flour** and add **1 cup sauerkraut cooking liquid.** Cook and stir until smooth. Mix with sauerkraut and peas; heat thoroughly.

Stewed Sauerkraut with Mushrooms
(Kapusta Kiszona z Grzybami)

1 ounce dried mushrooms or ¼
    pound fresh mushrooms
½ cup warm water
1 large onion, diced
2½ tablespoons butter or shortening
1½ pounds sauerkraut, rinsed and
    drained
⅓ cup water
2 tablespoons flour
    Salt and pepper

1. Soak the dried mushrooms in ½ cup warm water 1 hour.
2. Sauté mushrooms and onion in butter in a skillet 3 minutes.
3. Add sauerkraut to mushrooms; cook and stir 10 minutes.
4. Blend ⅓ cup water into flour. Mix with sauerkraut and simmer 15 minutes. Season to taste with salt and pepper. Serve with **fish.**

About 6 servings

Holiday tradition demands a pungent beet relish at all festive occasions, especially Christmas and Easter.

Pickled Beets *(Ćwikła)*

3 cups sliced cooked or canned
    beets
1 tablespoon grated fresh
    horseradish or 4 teaspoons
    prepared horseradish
8 whole cloves or ½ teaspoon
    caraway seed
2 cups vinegar
1 tablespoon brown sugar
2 teaspoons salt

1. Layer beets in a glass or earthenware bowl, sprinkling layers with horseradish and cloves.
2. Boil vinegar with sugar and salt 2 minutes. Pour over the beets. Cover; refrigerate 24 hours.

About 3 cups

Mushrooms with Sour Cream
(Grzybki z Kwaśną Śmietaną)

1 large onion, minced
2 tablespoons butter
1 pound fresh mushrooms, diced
1 tablespoon flour
½ teaspoon salt
¼ teaspoon pepper
½ cup whipping cream
½ cup dairy sour cream
¼ cup grated cheese (Parmesan,
    Swiss, or Cheddar)
2 tablespoons butter, melted

1. Sauté onion in 2 tablespoons butter in a skillet 5 minutes. Add mushrooms; sauté 5 minutes longer.
2. Blend flour, salt, and pepper with skillet mixture. Add whipping cream and sour cream gradually; mixing thoroughly. Turn into 1-quart casserole. Top with cheese. Drizzle melted butter over top.
3. Bake at 350°F about 20 minutes, or until thoroughly heated.

4 to 6 servings

Egg Noodles with Poppy Seed
(Kluski z Makiem)

1½ quarts boiling water
1 teaspoon salt
3 cups egg noodles
½ cup milk
½ cup poppy seed, ground
3 tablespoons sugar or 2
    tablespoons honey

1. Combine boiling water and salt in a large saucepan. Add noodles and cook until tender. Drain.
2. Meanwhile, scald milk; mix in poppy seed and sugar. Cook 5 minutes.
3. Combine poppy seed mixture with the noodles. Serve hot.

4 to 6 servings

Noodles with Poppy Seed and Raisins
(Kluski z Makiem i Rodzynkami)

2 cups cooked egg noodles
2 tablespoons butter, melted
1 can (12 ounces) poppy seed cake
    and pastry filling
1 teaspoon vanilla extract
1 teaspoon lemon juice
1½ teaspoons grated lemon peel
⅓ cup raisins

1. Toss noodles with butter in a saucepan.
2. Combine poppy seed filling with vanilla extract, lemon juice and peel, and raisins. Add to noodles and mix well. Cook just until heated through.

About 6 servings.

Pancakes, pierogi, kolduny, and other filled noodles are popular on Christmas Eve tables. Choose a favorite noodle form for these tasty, nonmeat fillings.

Mushroom Filling

1 can (8 ounces) mushrooms,
    drained
1 large onion, chopped
3 tablespoons butter or margarine
3 tablespoons dry bread crumbs
¼ teaspoon salt
¼ teaspoon pepper

1. Stir-fry mushrooms and onion in butter in a heavy skillet until onion is transparent.
2. Finely chop, or grind, the mushrooms and onion. Stir in remaining ingredients.

About 1½ cups

Spinach Filling

2 pounds fresh spinach or 2
    packages (10 ounces each)
    frozen chopped spinach
1 onion, chopped

1. Wash the spinach very well. Remove tough stems.
2. Put spinach into a saucepan with only the water clinging to the leaves. Cover and cook rapidly 5 minutes. (Cook frozen spinach following package directions.) Drain.

2 tablespoons butter
2 tablespoons grated Parmesan
   cheese
2 tablespoons bread crumbs
   Salt and pepper

3. Chop spinach and force through a sieve or purée in an electric blender.
4. Fry the onion in butter until golden.
5. Combine the spinach, onion, cheese, and bread crumbs; mix well. Season to taste with salt and pepper.

About 3 cups

Traditionally served in the southeastern provinces of Poland on Christmas Eve.

Christmas Eve "Kutia" (Kutia Wigilijna)

1 cup cracked wheat or bulgur
2 cups hot water
1 cup honey
2 cups water
1 teaspoon salt

1. Soak wheat in 2 cups hot water 30 minutes. Bring to boiling; cook covered until tender.
2. Cook honey with remaining 2 cups water 20 minutes. Add salt. Cool and serve with wheat.

About 4 servings

Christmas Cake

3 cups all-purpose flour
2 cups sugar
2 teaspoons baking soda
1 teaspoon allspice
1 teaspoon cinnamon
1 teaspoon nutmeg
1 teaspoon cloves
1 teaspoon salt
⅔ cup butter or margarine
2 cups buttermilk
1 cup chopped dates, raisins, or
   mixed candied fruits
½ cup chopped almonds or walnuts

1. Combine flour, sugar, baking soda, spices, and salt in a bowl. Cut in butter with pastry blender or two knives until particles resemble rice kernels. Add buttermilk; mix thoroughly. Mix in dates and nuts.
2. Turn batter into a generously greased and floured (bottom only) 9-inch tube pan or into two 8×4×3-inch loaf pans.
3. Bake at 350°F about 1 hour, or until a wooden pick comes out clean.
4. Cool in pan on wire rack 15 minutes. Remove from pan and cool completely on wire rack.

1 tube cake

Marzipan (Marcepan)

1 pound blanched almonds
1 pound confectioners' sugar
2 tablespoons orange water or rose
   water
   Food coloring
   Decorations (colored sugar,
      dragées, or chocolate shot)

1. Grind almonds very fine. Combine in a saucepan with sugar and flavoring. Cook until mixture leaves side of pan.
2. Roll almond mixture on flat surface to ½-inch thickness. Cut out small heart shapes. Or, shape into small fruits or vegetables.
3. Paint with appropriate food coloring or coat as desired, for example, with red sugar for "strawberries" and cocoa for "potatoes." Decorate with dragées or chocolate shot. Place on waxed paper to dry 2 hours.

2 pounds

Poppy Seed Rolls *(Strucle z Makiem)*

Dough:
- 2 packages active dry yeast
- ½ cup warm water
- 4½ cups all-purpose flour
- ¾ cup sugar
- ½ teaspoon salt
- ½ cup butter or margarine
- 2 eggs
- 2 egg yolks
- ½ cup dairy sour cream
- 1 teaspoon vanilla extract

Filling:
- 2 tablespoons butter
- 10 ounces poppy seed, ground twice (may be purchased already ground in gourmet shops)
- 2 tablespoons honey
- 2 teaspoons lemon juice or vanilla extract
- ¼ cup raisins, steamed
- 2 egg whites
- ½ cup sugar
- ¼ cup finely chopped candied orange peel
- 2 teaspoons grated lemon peel

Icing:
- 1 cup confectioners' sugar
- 2 tablespoons lemon juice

1. For dough, soften yeast in warm water in a bowl.
2. Mix flour with sugar and salt. Cut in butter with a pastry blender or two knives until mixture has a fine, even crumb.
3. Beat eggs and egg yolks; mix with yeast, then stir into flour mixture. Add sour cream and vanilla extract; mix well.
4. Knead dough on floured surface for 5 minutes. Divide in half. Roll each half of dough into a 12-inch square. Cover.
5. For filling, melt butter in a large saucepan. Add poppy seed. Stir-fry 3 minutes.
6. Add honey, lemon juice, and raisins to poppy seed. Cover and remove from heat; let stand 10 minutes.
7. Beat egg whites with sugar until stiff, not dry, peaks form. Fold in orange and lemon peels. Gently fold in poppy seed mixture.
8. Spread half of filling over each square of dough. Roll up, jelly-roll fashion. Seal edges. Place on greased baking sheets. Cover. Let rise until doubled in bulk, about 1½ hours.
9. Bake at 350°F about 45 minutes. Cool.
10. For icing, blend sugar and lemon juice until smooth. Spread over rolls.

2 poppy seed rolls

Christmas Bread *(Placek Świąteczny)*

- 5 eggs
- 2 cups confectioners' sugar
- 2¼ cups all-purpose flour
- ¾ cup finely chopped walnuts
- ⅔ cup raisins
- 4 ounces candied orange peel, finely chopped
- 2 teaspoons baking powder
- ½ teaspoon salt
- 1 cup butter or margarine (at room temperature)
- 1 tablespoon grated lemon peel
- 1 teaspoon vanilla extract
- 3 tablespoons vodka or brandy

1. Beat eggs with sugar 5 minutes at high speed of electric mixer.
2. Mix nuts, raisins, and orange peel with 2 tablespoons flour. Mix remaining flour with baking powder and salt.
3. Cream butter, lemon peel, and vanilla extract until fluffy. Beat in vodka. Add egg mixture gradually, beating constantly. Add flour mixture and beat 5 minutes. Fold fruit-nut mixture into the batter. Turn into a generously greased and floured 9×5×3-inch loaf pan or 1½-quart ring mold.
4. Bake at 350°F 1 hour.
5. Cool cake in pan on wire rack 10 minutes. Turn cake out onto rack; cool completely.
6. Wrap in plastic wrap. Store 1 or 2 days to mellow. Sprinkle with confectioners' sugar, if desired, or ice with Lemon Icing (page 70).

1 loaf

Light Fruitcake from Warsaw
(Keks Warszawski)

5 eggs or 3 whole eggs plus 3 egg whites
1¾ cups confectioners' sugar
¾ cup butter
1 teaspoon vanilla extract
¼ cup milk or brandy
½ teaspoon salt
3 cups sifted cake flour
2 teaspoons baking powder
3 ounces candied orange peel, finely chopped (about ¾ cup)
⅔ cup currants or raisins
⅔ cup finely chopped walnuts
½ cup sliced dried figs
½ cup diced pitted dried prunes
½ tablespoon cornstarch

1. Beat eggs with sugar at high speed of electric mixer 7 minutes.
2. Cream butter with vanilla extract until fluffy. Beat in milk and salt.
3. Mix half of flour with baking powder. Add to creamed mixture and mix thoroughly. Fold in beaten eggs, then remaining flour.
4. Mix fruits and nuts with cornstarch. Fold into batter.
5. Butter an 11×7×3-inch loaf pan and sprinkle with bread crumbs. Turn batter into pan.
6. Bake at 350°F 50 minutes, or until a wooden pick comes out clean.
7. Cool before slicing.

1 fruitcake

Baked Apples with Red Wine
(Jabłka na Winie Czerwonym)

8 apples, cored
Cherry or strawberry preserves
½ cup sugar
½ teaspoon mace or nutmeg
1 cup red wine
½ teaspoon vanilla extract

1. Place apples in a buttered casserole or baking dish. Fill each with preserves.
2. Blend sugar and mace; stir in wine and vanilla extract. Pour over apples. Cover.
3. Bake at 350°F 1 hour.
4. Chill 2 to 4 hours before serving.

8 servings

Twelve-Fruit Compote

3 cups water
1 pound mixed dried fruits including pears, figs, apricots, and peaches
1 cup pitted prunes
½ cup raisins or currants
1 cup pitted sweet cherries
2 apples, peeled and sliced or 6 ounces dried apple slices
½ cup cranberries
1 cup sugar
1 lemon, sliced
6 whole cloves
2 cinnamon sticks (3 inches each)
1 orange
½ cup grapes, pomegranate seeds, or pitted plums
½ cup fruit-flavored brandy

1. Combine water, mixed dried fruits, prunes, and raisins in a 6-quart kettle. Bring to boiling. Cover; simmer about 20 minutes, or until fruits are plump and tender.
2. Add cherries, apples, and cranberries. Stir in sugar, lemon, and spices. Cover; simmer 5 minutes.
3. Grate peel of orange; reserve. Peel and section orange, removing all skin and white membrane. Add to fruits in kettle.
4. Stir in grapes and brandy. Bring just to boiling. Remove from heat. Stir in orange peel. Cover; let stand 15 minutes.

About 12 servings

INDEX

Anchovies
 chicken with, 54
 eggs with, 77
 pike or carp stuffed with, 46
 purée of, 18
 roast turkey with, 55
Appetizers
 beet relish, 13
 dill pickles, 15
 eggs with anchovies, 77
 feet in aspic, 14
 flybanes, 16
 fresh mushrooms in sour cream, 15
 ham
  and egg rolls, 16
  pudding, 16
 pâté
  pork, 15
  turkey, 77
  veal, 77
 pickled
  herring in sour cream, 87
  mushrooms, 13
  watermelon rind, 14

Baba, 72
 au rhum, 72
 Easter, 80
 filled, 72
 with raisins, 80
Bacon fry, 52
Barley
 egg, 30
 soup, 22
Beef
 filling, 38
 hussar roast, 41
 pot roast, 42
  with sour cream, 42
  with sour cream and pickles or mushrooms, 42
 slices with sour cream and mushrooms, 42
 steamed, 42
Beet(s)
 kvas, 19
 pickled, 89
 red, with horseradish, 79
 relish, 13
 soup
  cold cucumber-, 25
  volhynian, 25
Borscht
 clear, 26
 with meat, 24

without meat, 87
Brains filling, 39
Bread(s)
 Christmas, 92
 croutons, 30
 croutons for fruit soups, 29
 dark rye, 29
 poppy seed rolls, 92
Broth
 chicken, 23
 fish, 23
 meat, 24
Butter
 mustard, 17
 onion-chive, 18

Cabbage
 and mushroom filling with egg, 39
 braised lamb with savoy, 47
 Polish noodles and, 58
 red
  duck with, 55
  Polish sausage with, 51
 rolls, 52
  stuffed, 53
  with mushroom sauce, 52
 soup, fresh, 25
Cakes, see Desserts
Canapés, 16
Capon in cream, 56
Carp, see Fish
Chicken
 broth, 23
 livers in Madeira sauce, 49
 liver spread, 18
 Polish style, 54
 royal, 53
 smothered stuffed, 54
 with anchovies, 54
 with ham, 54
Chocolate torte, 70
Christmas
 bread, 92
 cake, 91
 eve "kutia," 91
Compote(s)
 berry, 74
 fruit, in spirits, 74
 pear, 74
 pear and apple, 74
 twelve-fruit, 93
Cookies, see Desserts
Croquettes, 31
Croutons, 30
 for fruit soups, 29

Desserts
 apples in blankets, 73
 baba
  au rhum, 72
  Easter, 80

filled, 72
 with raisins, 80
 baked apples with red wine, 93
 black bread pudding, 70
 butter horns, 65
 cakes
  apple, 71
  Christmas, 91
  cross, 83
  lamb, 81
  plum, 71
 cheese cake, 73
  Easter, 82
  grandmother's, 81
 cheese pascha from Lwow, 82
 Christmas eve "kutia," 91
 compotes
  berry, 74
  fruit, in spirits, 74
  pear, 74
  pear and apple, 74
  twelve-fruit, 93
 cookies
  butter horns, 65
  honey, 67
  Polish pecan, 65
 doughnuts, Polish, 66
 favors, 66
 fruitcake from Warsaw, light, 93
 kolacky, 67
 marzipan, 91
 mazurkas, 68
  almond, 68
  royal, 68
  with apple topping, 69
  with chocolate topping, 69
  with fruit and nut topping, 69
  with lemon icing, 70
 pączki, excellent Warsaw, 84
 raspberry syrup, 73
 tortes
  chocolate, 70
  walnut, 71
 wise men, 66
Duck
 in caper sauce, smothered, 55
 soup, 21
 wild, 57
 with red cabbage, 55
Dumplings
 egg
  balls, 32
  barley, 30
  drops, 31
 fish, 32
 potato, 31
 raw potato, 32
 string, 31
 suet or marrow balls, 31

Easter
 baba, 80

cheese cake, 82
soup, 78
Eel, roulade of, 45
Egg(s)
balls, 32
barley, 30
crowns, 77
drops, 31
flybanes, 16
rolls, ham and, 16
with anchovies, 77

Filling(s)
beef, 38
brains, 39
cabbage and mushroom, with
egg, 39
cheese
savory, 40
sweet, 40
cooked
fruit, 40
meat, 38
fruit, 69
meat, 38
mushroom, 39, 90
potato, 39
prune, 40
sauerkraut, 39
sauerkraut and mushroom, 40
sausage, 38
spinach, 90
Fingers
stuffed yeast, 37
yeast, 37
Fish, 43
au gratin, 45
with horseradish, 45
with mushrooms, 45
with tomatoes, 45
baked leftover, 44
broth, 23
dumplings, 32
in Greek sauce, 47
in horseradish sauce, 88
northern pike Polish style, 46
pike or carp stuffed with anchovies, 46
sole with vegetables, 44
stuffed baked, 46
Flour, browned, 56
Flybanes, 16
Frosting
butter
basic, 83
cream decorating, 83
lemon, 83
orange, 83
for chocolate torte, 70
for walnut torte, 71
seven-minute, 81

Fruit(s)
baked apples with red wine, 93
compotes
berry, 74
fruit, in spirits, 74
pear, 74
pear and apple, 74
twelve-fruit, 93
fillings, 40
soups, 26
soups, croutons for, 29

Goose, wild, 57

Ham
and egg rolls, 16
chicken with, 54
in rye crust, 78
pudding, 16
Herring, pickled, in sour cream, 87

Icing, lemon, 70

Kolacky, 67
Kołduny, 34
Kulebiak, 34
"Kutia," Christmas eve, 91
Kvas
beet, 19
bread, 19
rye flour, 19

Lamb
braised, with caraway seed, 47
braised, with savoy cabbage, 47
Little ears, 33, 36
Liver(s)
à la Nelson, 50
chicken, in Madeira sauce, 49
mounds, 32
spread, chicken, 18

Marrow balls, suet or, 31
Marzipan, 91
Mazurkas, 68
almond, 68
with apple topping, 69
with chocolate topping, 69
with fruit and nut topping, 69
with lemon icing, 70
Mushroom(s)
cutlets, 59
filling, 39, 90
sauerkraut and, 40
with egg, cabbage and, 39
in sour cream, fresh, 15
mounds, baked, 59
pickled, 13
sauce, 64
soup, 20
stewed sauerkraut with, 89
with sour cream, 89

Mustard
butter, 17
sauce, 63

Naleśniki, 34, 36
Noodles
and cabbage, Polish, 58
beaten, 30
chiffon, 30
egg, 31
egg, with poppy seed, 90
little ears, 36
pierogi, 36
rice, 30
with poppy seed and raisins, 90
yeast pierogi, 35

Paczki, excellent Warsaw, 84
Pancakes, 34
thick, 37
thin, 36
Partridge, wild, 57
Pascha from Lwow, cheese, 82
Pâté
pork, 15
turkey, 77
veal, 77
Pheasant, potted, 56
Pickle(s)
dill, 15
dill, soup, 21
Pierogi, 33, 36
yeast, 35
Pigeon(s)
baked, 57
smothered, 56
Pig('s)
feet in aspic, 14
roast suckling, 79
Pike, see Fish
Pork
pâté, 15
pot roast, 49
roast loin of, 48
sauerkraut with, 48
Poultry, see specific kinds
Puddings, see Desserts

Rabbit, 57
Relish
beet, 13
pickled beets, 89
Rice noodles, 30

Salad(s)
potato, with wine, 63
rose, 63
sauerkraut, with carrots and apples, 62
Warsaw, 62
Sauce(s)
caper, smothered duck in, 55

Greek, fish in, 47
green onion, 64
horseradish
   cold, 64
   fish in, 88
Madeira, chicken livers in, 49
mushroom, 64
mushroom, cabbage rolls with, 52
mustard, 63
Polish, sausage in, 51
sour cream, 64
tartar, 64
Sauerkraut, 60
   and mushroom filling, 40
   filling, 39
   salad with carrots and apples, 62
   soup, 23
   stewed, with mushrooms, 89
   with dried peas
      for Christmas Eve, 88
      for nonfast days, 88
   with pork, 48
Sausage
   filling, 38
   in Polish sauce, 51
   Polish, 78
   Polish, with red cabbage, 51
Sole, see Fish
Soup(s)
   almond, 87
   barley, 22
   beer, 26
   black bread, 22
   borscht
      clear, 26
      with meat, 24
      without meat, 87
   broth
      chicken, 23
      fish, 23
      meat, 24
   cabbage, fresh, 25
   caraway, 22
   cucumber-beet, cold, 25
   dill pickle, 21
   duck, 21

Easter, 78
fruit
   apple, 26
   apricot, 27
   berry, 27
   cherry, 28
   croutons for, 29
   plum, 27
   prune, 27
kvas
   beet, 19
   bread, 19
   rye flour, 19
mushroom, 20
"nothing," 20
pumpkin, 20
sauerkraut, 23
volhynian beet, 25
wine, 26
Spread(s)
   chicken liver, 18
   spring cottage cheese, 18
Stew(s)
   easy hunter's, 28
   hunter's, 28
Stock, meat, 24
Stuffing, 41
Suckling pig, roast, 79
Suet or marrow balls, 31
Syrup, raspberry, 73

Tongue, boiled, 50
Toppings
   apple, 69
   chocolate, 69
   nut, 69
Tripe and vegetables Warsaw style, 50
Turkey
   pâté, 77
   roast, with anchovies, 55

Uszka, 33, 36

Veal
   à la Nelson, 58

pâté, 77
roasted, 79
Vegetables
   artichokes or tomatoes, stuffed, 62
   beets, 59
      pickled, 89
      red, with horseradish, 79
   cabbage
      braised lamb with savoy, 47
      duck with red, 55
      Polish noodles and, 58
      Polish sausage with red, 51
      rolls, 52
      rolls, stuffed, 53
      rolls with mushroom sauce, 52
   croquettes, 31
   cucumbers in sour cream, 60
   green peas or salad greens, smothered, 61
   polonaise, 60
   radishes with sour cream, 60
   sauerkraut, 60
      salad with carrots and apples, 62
      stewed, with mushrooms, 89
      with dried peas (for Christmas Eve), 88
      with dried peas (for nonfast days), 88
      with pork, 48
   smothered, 61
   stuffed, 61
   tomatoes, stuffed, 60
Venison, leg of, 58
Vodka, fire, 84
Volhynian beet soup, 25

Walnut torte, 71
Watermelon rind, pickled, 14

Yeast
   fingers, 37
   fingers, stuffed, 37
   pierogi, 35